P9-DWH-194

THE
YOGA
OF JESUS

Understanding the Hidden Teachings of the Gospels

Selections from the writings of

Paramahansa Yogananda

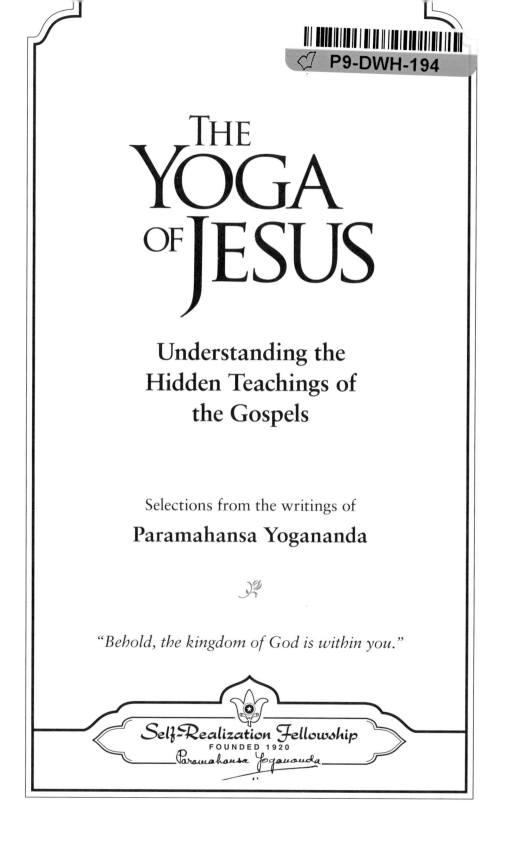

"Behold, the kingdom of God is within you."

Self-Realization Fellowship
FOUNDED 1920
Paramahansa Yogananda

Copyright © 2007 Self-Realization Fellowship

First edition, 2007. This printing, 2011.

All rights reserved. Except for brief quotations in book reviews, and as otherwise permitted by applicable law, no part of this work may be reproduced, stored, transmitted or displayed in any form, or by any means (electronic, mechanical, or otherwise) now known or hereafter devised—including photocopy, recording, or any information storage and retrieval system—without prior written permission from Self-Realization Fellowship, Los Angeles, California 90065-3219, U.S.A.

 Authorized by the International Publications Council of Self-Realization Fellowship

The Self-Realization Fellowship name and emblem (shown above) appear on all SRF books, recordings, and other publications, assuring the reader that a work originates with the society established by Paramahansa Yogananda and faithfully conveys his teachings.

Library of Congress Cataloging-in-Publication Data

Yogananda, Paramahansa, 1893–1952
[Selections. 2007. Self-Realization Fellowship]
The yoga of Jesus : understanding the hidden teachings of the gospels : selections from the writings of Paramahansa Yogananda. —1st ed.
p. cm.
Includes index.
Summary: "Contains selected excerpts from Paramahansa Yogananda's book "The Second Coming of Christ: The Resurrection of the Christ Within You," which book is a commentary on the New Testament gospels and noncanonical source material, focusing on the quest to uncover the original teachings of Jesus"—Provided by publisher.
ISBN 978-0-87612-556-4 (pbk. : alk. paper)
1. Jesus Christ—Oriental interpretations. 2. Christianity and yoga. I. Title.
BT304.94.Y63 2007
294.5'2—dc22

2007032915
Printed in the United States of America
1730-J1990

Contents

Part III: Jesus' Yoga of Divine Love

A note to the reader:

To assist the reader who may be unfamiliar with the concepts and terminology of Yoga and Eastern philosophy, a glossary has been provided at the back of the book.

This gives easy-to-find definitions of most of the terms that are important to understanding Paramahansa Yogananda's exposition of the teachings of Jesus—such as Christ Consciousness, Holy Ghost, *Aum*, the astral and causal worlds, and the various yogic terms applicable to the experience of meditation and God-realization.

Preface

- *Did Jesus, like the ancient sages and masters of the East, teach meditation as the way to enter "the kingdom of heaven"?*

- *Were there "hidden teachings" given to his immediate disciples, which have been lost or suppressed through the centuries?*

- *Did he really teach that all non-Christians are excluded from God's kingdom? And does a literal reading of the Gospel truly probe the depths of his epoch-making message for humanity?*

These and other questions are answered with reverent understanding and unprecedented insight by Paramahansa Yogananda in *The Second Coming of Christ: The Resurrection of the Christ Within You.* And his conclusions tally remarkably with contemporary religious scholars' ongoing explorations of the profound esoteric and experiential dimensions of early Christianity, as revealed in the "Gnostic gospels" and other recently discovered manuscripts lost since the second and third centuries.

Paramahansa Yogananda is renowned as "the Father of Yoga in the West" and one of the preeminent spiritual figures of our time. *The Second Coming of Christ*—his monumental work on the "original teachings of Jesus"—was published in two large volumes (totaling more than 1,700 pages) in 2004. Taking the reader verse by verse through the four Gospels, the book's 75 discourses provide in-depth discussions of the true significance of Jesus' words, showing how they can only be fully understood when considered in the light of their original purpose: as a path to direct, personal experience of "the kingdom of God within you."

Reporting on the release of this groundbreaking work, the *Los Angeles Times* (December 11, 2004) wrote: "*The Second Coming of Christ: The Resurrection of the Christ Within You* offers startling ideas about the deeper meaning of Jesus' teachings and their essential unity with yoga, one of the world's oldest and most systematic religious paths to achieving oneness with God....The book aims to recover what Yoga-nanda believed were major teachings lost to institutional Christianity. Among them was the idea that every seeker can know God not through mere belief but by direct experience via yoga meditation."

Another review, in *Sacred Pathways* magazine (December 2004), stated: "Yogananda strips away the divisiveness and dogmatic approach that have accumulated around Jesus' teachings and affirms that it is possible for every individual—regardless of one's faith tradition—to have the same relationship that Jesus had with the Divine....He outlines the methods of God-communion that Jesus imparted to his direct disciples but which were obscured over the centuries, and explains such topics as the Holy Ghost, baptism, meditation, forgiveness of sins, reincarnation, heaven and hell, and resurrection. In so doing, he reveals the underlying unity of Jesus' moral and esoteric teachings with India's ancient science of Yoga, meditation, and union with God."

Experts in the fields of religion, history, and healing also praised the book: "This is one of those rare bridge-building books that can truly change the way one sees a figure one thought one knew well," wrote Dr. Robert Ellwood, Emeritus Professor of Religion, University of Southern California.

"Paramahansa Yogananda's *The Second Coming of Christ* is one of the most important analyses of Jesus' teachings that exists," said Dr. Larry Dossey, M.D., noted author and researcher in the field of holistic medicine. "Many interpretations of Jesus's words divide peoples, cultures, and nations; these foster unity and healing, and that is why they are vital for today's world."

Yoga International magazine (March 2005) began its review of the book with these words: "Yoga went global in the twentieth century. Now it seems likely that the divisive chasm between Christian teaching and India's ancient spiritual science will finally be bridged here in the twentyfirst. Paramahansa Yogananda's new book, *The Second Coming of Christ,* holds out this promise, arguing that the division has always been superficial. The implications for yoga practitioners in the West—and for society at large—are enormous."

This present volume is intended as a first glimpse of Paramahansa Yogananda's revelatory exposition on the hidden yoga of the Gospels, which is explained in much greater detail in *The Second Coming of Christ.*

What Is Yoga, Really?

Most of us are accustomed to looking outside of ourselves for fulfillment. We are living in a world that conditions us to believe that outer attainments can give us what we want. Yet again and again our experiences show us that nothing external can completely fulfill the deep longing within for "something more."

Most of the time, however, we find ourselves striving toward that which always seems to lie just beyond our reach. We are caught up in *doing* rather than *being,* in *action* rather than *awareness.* It is hard for us to picture a state of complete calmness and repose in which thoughts and feelings cease to dance in perpetual motion. Yet it is through such a state of quietude that we can touch a level of joy and understanding impossible to achieve otherwise.

It is said in the Bible: "Be still, and know that I am God." In these few words lies the key to the science of yoga. This ancient spiritual science offers a direct means of stilling the natural turbulence of thoughts and restlessness of body that prevent us from knowing what we really are.

Ordinarily our awareness and energies are directed outward, to the things of this world, which we perceive through the limited instruments of our five senses. Because human reason has to rely upon the partial and often deceptive data supplied by the physical senses, we must learn to tap deeper and more subtle levels of awareness if we would solve the enigmas of life—*Who am I? Why am I here? How do I realize Truth?*

Yoga is a simple process of reversing the ordinary outward flow of energy and consciousness so that the mind becomes a dynamic center of direct perception—no longer dependent upon the fallible senses but capable of actually experiencing Truth.

By practicing the step-by-step methods of yoga—taking nothing for granted on emotional grounds or through blind faith—we come to know our oneness with the Infinite Intelligence, Power, and Joy which gives life to all and which is the essence of our own Self.*

In past centuries many of the higher techniques of yoga were little understood or practiced, owing to mankind's limited knowledge of the forces that run the universe. But today scientific investigation is rapidly changing the way we view ourselves and the world. The traditional materialistic conception of life has vanished with the discovery that matter and energy are essentially one: Every existing substance can be reduced to a pattern or form of energy, which interacts and interconnects with other forms. Some of today's most celebrated physicists go a step further, identifying *consciousness* as the fundamental ground of all being. Thus modern science is confirming the ancient principles of yoga, which proclaim that unity pervades the universe.

The word *yoga* itself means "union": of the individual consciousness or soul with the Universal Consciousness or Spirit. Though many people think of yoga only as physical exercises—the *asanas* or postures that have gained widespread popularity in recent decades—these are actually only the most superficial aspect of this profound science of unfolding the infinite potentials of the human mind and soul.

There are various paths of yoga that lead toward this goal, each one a specialized branch of one comprehensive system:

Hatha Yoga—a system of physical postures, or *asanas*, whose higher purpose is to purify the body, giving one awareness and control over its internal states and rendering it fit for meditation.

Karma Yoga—selfless service to others as part of one's larger Self, without attachment to the results; and the performance of all actions with the consciousness of God as the Doer.

Mantra Yoga—centering the consciousness within through *japa*, or the repetition of certain universal root-word sounds representing a particular aspect of Spirit.

Bhakti Yoga—all-surrendering devotion through which one strives

---

* "Self" is capitalized to denote the soul, man's true identity, in contradistinction to the ego or pseudo-soul, the lower self with which man temporarily identifies through ignorance of his real nature.

to see and love the divinity in every creature and in everything, thus maintaining an unceasing worship.

Jnana Yoga—the path of wisdom, which emphasizes the application of discriminative intelligence to achieve spiritual liberation.

Raja Yoga—the royal or highest path of yoga, formally systematized in the second century B.C. by the Indian sage Patanjali, which combines the essence of all the other paths.

At the heart of the Raja Yoga system, balancing and unifying these various approaches, is the practice of definite, scientific methods of meditation that enable one to perceive, from the very beginning of one's efforts, glimpses of the ultimate goal—conscious union with the inexhaustibly blissful Spirit.

The quickest and most effective approach to the goal of yoga employs those methods of meditation that deal directly with energy and consciousness. It is this direct approach that characterizes *Kriya Yoga,** the particular form of Raja Yoga meditation taught by Paramahansa Yogananda.

India's most beloved scripture of yoga is the Bhagavad Gita—a profound treatise on union with God, and a timeless prescription for happiness and balanced success in everyday life. That Jesus knew and taught the same universal science of God-realization and precepts for spiritual living is the revelation brought to the world at large by Paramahansa Yogananda, as shown in the pages of this book.†

A brief work such as the present one can provide only an introductory glimpse of the profound and inspiring unity between the teachings of Jesus the Christ and those of yoga. Readers who are inspired by this selection of

---

* *"Kriya* is an ancient science," Paramahansa Yogananda wrote in his *Autobiography of a Yogi.* "Lahiri Mahasaya received it from his great guru, Babaji, who rediscovered and clarified the technique after it had been lost in the Dark Ages. Babaji renamed it, simply, *Kriya Yoga.*"

"The *Kriya Yoga* that I am giving to the world through you in this nineteenth century," Babaji told Lahiri Mahasaya, "is a revival of the same science that Krishna gave millenniums ago to Arjuna; and that was later known to Patanjali and Christ, and to St. John, St. Paul, and other disciples."

† A small companion volume, *The Yoga of the Bhagavad Gita: An Introduction to India's Universal Science of God-Realization,* has been published simultaneously with the present book— excerpts from the comprehensive teachings of the Gita presented in Paramahansa Yogananda's highly acclaimed two-volume commentary, *God Talks With Arjuna: The Bhagavad Gita.*

excerpts will find abundantly more detail and practical teaching for daily life in the two volumes of *The Second Coming of Christ*. As Paramahansa Yogananda writes in the introduction to that work:

"In these pages I offer to the world an intuitionally perceived spiritual interpretation of the words spoken by Jesus, truths received through actual communion with Christ Consciousness. They will be found to be universally true if they are studied conscientiously and meditated upon with soul-awakened intuitive perception. They reveal the perfect unity that exists among the revelations of the Christian Bible, the Bhagavad Gita of India, and all other time-tested true scriptures.

"The saviors of the world do not come to foster inimical doctrinal divisions; their teachings should not be used toward that end. It is something of a misnomer even to refer to the New Testament as the 'Christian' Bible, for it does not belong exclusively to any one sect. Truth is meant for the blessing and upliftment of the entire human race. As the Christ Consciousness is universal, so does Jesus Christ belong to all."

—Self-Realization Fellowship

PART I

---◆◇◆---

JESUS THE CHRIST— AVATAR AND YOGI

---◆◇◆---

"Do you believe in the divinity of Christ?"
a visitor inquired.

Paramahansa Yogananda replied: "Yes.
I love to talk of him because he was a man
of perfect Self-realization. However, he was
not the only *son of God, nor did he claim to*
be. Instead, he clearly taught that those who
do the will of God become, like himself, one
with Him.

"Wasn't it the mission of Jesus on earth
to remind all men that the Lord is their
Heavenly Father, and to show them the way
back to Him?"

—Sayings of Paramahansa Yogananda

CHAPTER 1

Jesus the Avatar

God's Manifestation in Divine Incarnations

For mere mortals to cope with a life of unsolved and unsolvable mysteries in an inscrutable universe would indeed be an overwhelming challenge were it not for divine emissaries who come on earth to speak with the voice and authority of God for the guidance of man.

Aeons past, in ancient higher ages in India, *rishis* enunciated the manifestation of Divine Beneficence, of "God with us," in terms of divine incarnations, avatars—God incarnate on earth in enlightened beings....

Many are the voices that have intermediated between God and man, *khanda avatars*, or partial incarnations in God-knowing souls. Less common are the *purna avatars*, liberated beings who are fully one with God; their return to earth is to fulfill a God-ordained mission.

The Lord in the sacred Hindu Bible, the Bhagavad Gita, declares:

"Whenever virtue declines and vice predominates, I incarnate as an Avatar. In visible form I appear from age to age to protect the virtuous and to destroy evildoing in order to reestablish righteousness."

The same one glorious infinite consciousness of God, the Universal Christ Consciousness, *Kutastha Chaitanya*, becomes familiarly apparelled in the individuality of an enlightened soul, graced with a distinguishing personality and godly nature appropriate to the times and purpose of the incarnation.

Without this intercession of God's love come to earth in the example, message, and guiding hand of His avatars, it would scarce be possible for groping humanity to find the path into God's kingdom midst the dark miasma of world delusion, the cosmic substance of human habitation.

3

Lest His benighted children be lost forever in creation's delusive laby-
rinths, the Lord comes again and again in God-illumined prophets to
light the way....

Jesus was preceded by Gautama Buddha, the "Enlightened One,"
whose incarnation reminded a forgetful generation of the Dharma
Chakra, the ever-rotating wheel of karma—self-initiated action and its
effects which make each man, and not a Cosmic Dictator, responsible
for his own present condition. Buddha brought heart back into the arid
theology and mechanical rituals into which the ancient Vedic religion
of India had fallen after the passing of a higher age in which Bhagavan
Krishna, India's most beloved of avatars, preached the way of divine love
and God-realization through the practice of the supreme spiritual science
of yoga, union with God.

❖ ❖ ❖

Divine intercession to mitigate the cosmic law of cause and effect
[karma], by which a man suffers from his errors, was at the heart of the
mission of love Jesus came to fulfill....

Jesus came to demonstrate the forgiveness and compassion of God,
whose love is a shelter even from exacting law.

❖ ❖ ❖

The Good Shepherd of souls opened his arms to all, rejecting none,
and with universal love coaxed the world to follow him on the path to
liberation through the example of his spirit of sacrifice, renunciation,
forgiveness, love for friend and enemy alike, and supreme love for God
above all else.

As the tiny babe in the manger at Bethlehem, and as the savior who
healed the sick and raised the dead and applied the salve of love on the
wounds of errors, the Christ in Jesus lived among men as one of them
that they too might learn to live like gods.

Christ Consciousness: Oneness With God's Infinite Intelligence and Bliss Pervading All Creation

To understand the magnitude of a divine incarnation, it is necessary to understand the source and nature of the consciousness that is incarnate in the avatar.

Jesus spoke of this consciousness when he proclaimed: "I and my Father are one" (John 10:30) and "I am in the Father, and the Father in me" (John 14:11). Those who unite their consciousness to God know both the transcendent and the immanent nature of Spirit—the singularity of the ever-existing, ever-conscious, ever-new Bliss of the Uncreate Absolute, and the myriad manifestations of His Being as the infinitude of forms into which He variegates Himself in the panorama of creation.

❖ ❖ ❖

There is a distinguishing difference of meaning between *Jesus* and *Christ*. His given name was Jesus; his honorific title was "Christ." In his little human body called Jesus was born the vast Christ Consciousness, the omniscient Intelligence of God omnipresent in every part and particle of creation.

❖ ❖ ❖

The universe is not the result merely of a fortuitous combination of vibrating forces and subatomic particles, as proposed by material scientists—a chance excrescence of solids, liquids, and gases into earth, oceans, atmosphere, plants, all harmoniously interrelated to provide a habitable home for human beings. Blind forces cannot organize themselves into intelligently structured objects. As human intelligence is needed to put water into the small square compartments of an ice tray to be frozen into cubes, so in the coalescence of vibration into progressively evolving forms throughout the universe we see the results of a hidden Immanent Intelligence.

❖ ❖ ❖

What could be more miraculous than the evident presence in every speck of creation of a Divine Intelligence? How the mighty tree emerges from a tiny seed. How countless worlds roll in infinite space, held in a purposeful cosmic dance by the precise adjustment of universal forces. How the marvelously complex human body is created from a single microscopic cell, is endowed with self-conscious intelligence, and

Science Discovers Intelligent Order

"The rise of science served to extend the range of nature's marvels, so that today we have discovered order in the deepest recesses of the atom and among the grandest collection of galaxies," writes Paul Davies, Ph.D., well-known author and professor of mathematical physics, in *Evidence of Purpose: Scientists Discover the Creator* (New York: Continuum Publishing, 1994).

Systems theorist Ervin Laszlo reports in *The Whispering Pond: A Personal Guide to the Emerging Vision of Science* (Boston: Element Books, 1999): "The fine-tuning of the physical universe to the parameters of life constitutes a series of coincidences — if that is what they are....in which even the slightest departure from the given values would spell the end of life, or, more exactly, create conditions under which life could never have evolved in the first place. If the neutron did not outweigh the proton in the nucleus of the atom, the active lifetime of the Sun and other stars would be reduced to a few hundred years; if the electric charge of electrons and protons did not balance precisely, all configurations of matter would be unstable and the universe would consist of nothing more than radiation and a relatively uniform mixture of gases....If the strong force that binds the particles of a nucleus were merely a fraction *weaker* than it is, deuteron could not exist and stars such as the Sun could not shine. And if that force were slightly *stronger* than it is, the Sun and other active stars would inflate and perhaps explode....The values of the four universal forces [electromagnetism, gravity, and the nuclear strong and weak forces] were precisely such that life could evolve in the cosmos."

Professor Davies estimates that if — as some scientists maintain — there were no inherent guiding intelligence and cosmic evolution were governed only by the chance operation of strictly mechanical laws, "the time required to achieve the level of order we now meet in the universe purely by random processes is of the order of at least $10^{10^{80}}$ years" — inconceivably longer than the current age of the universe. Citing these calculations, Laszlo wryly observes: "Serendipity of this magnitude strains credibility," and concludes: "Must we then face the possibility that the universe we witness is the result of purposeful design by an omnipotent master builder?" *(Publisher's Note)*

is sustained, healed, and enlivened by invisible power. In every atom of this astounding universe, God is ceaselessly working miracles; yet obtuse man takes them for granted.

❖ ❖ ❖

Christ is God's Infinite Intelligence that is present in all creation. The Infinite Christ is the "only begotten son" of God the Father, the only pure Reflection of Spirit in the created realm. That Universal Intelligence, the *Kutastha Chaitanya* or Krishna Consciousness of the Hindu scriptures, was fully manifested in the incarnation of Jesus, Krishna, and other divine ones; and it can be manifested also in your consciousness.

❖ ❖ ❖

Just imagine! If you were living in this one room all of your life, having no contact with or knowledge of what is beyond these walls, you would say that this is the whole of your world. But if someone were to take you into the world outside, you would realize how infinitesimal your "world" was. So it is with the perception of Christ Consciousness. The scope of mortal consciousness by comparison is like observing only the area of a tiny mustard seed to the exclusion of the rest of the cosmos. Christ Consciousness is Omnipresence, the Lord spread over every pore of infinite space and permeating every atom.*

❖ ❖ ❖

An ant's consciousness is limited to the sensations of its little body. An elephant's consciousness is extended throughout its massive frame, so that ten people touching ten different parts of its body would awaken simultaneous awareness. Christ Consciousness…extends to the boundaries of all vibratory regions.

The entirety of vibratory creation is an externalization of Spirit. Omnipresent Spirit secretes Itself in vibratory matter, just as oil is hidden in the olive. When the olive is squeezed, tiny drops of oil appear on its

* See also pages 24 ff. The counter-force in creation, which produces disharmony, disease, separateness, and ignorance, is personified in the Bible as Satan. In yoga philosophy this delusive force is called *Maya* or *Apara-Prakriti*. A comprehensive explanation is given by Paramahansa Yogananda in *The Second Coming of Christ: The Resurrection of the Christ Within You.*

surface; so Spirit, as individual souls, by a process of evolution gradually emerges from matter. Spirit expresses Itself as beauty and magnetic and chemical power in minerals and gems; as beauty and life in plants; as beauty, life, power, motion, and consciousness in animals; as comprehension and expanding power in man; and again returns to Omnipresence in the superman.*

Each evolutionary phase thus manifests a fuller measure of Spirit. The animal is freed from the inertia of minerals and the fixity of plants to experience with locomotion and sentient consciousness a greater portion of God's creation. Man, by his self-consciousness, additionally comprehends the thoughts of his fellow beings and can project his sensory mind into star-studded space, at least by the power of imagination.

The superman expands his life energy and consciousness from his body into all space, actually feeling as his own self the presence of all universes in the vast cosmos as well as every minute atom of the earth. In the superman, the lost omnipresence of Spirit, bound in the soul as individualized Spirit, is regained....

The consciousness of Jesus was transferred from the circumference of the body to the boundary of all finite creation in the vibratory region of manifestation: the sphere of space and time encompassing planetary universes, stars, the Milky Way, and our little solar system family of which the earth is a part, and on which the physical body of Jesus was but a speck. Jesus the man, a tiny particle on the earth, became Jesus the Christ, with his consciousness all-pervading in oneness with the Christ Consciousness.

Jesus' Principal Teaching: How to Become a Christ

God's work in creation is to draw, through evolutionary promptings of the Christ Intelligence, all beings back to conscious oneness with Himself....When there is widespread suffering on earth, God responds to the soul call of His devotees by sending a divine son who by his exemplary spiritual life of expressing Christ Consciousness can teach people

---

* These five evolutionary stages are referenced in yoga philosophy as *koshas,* "sheaths" that are progressively unfolded as creation evolves from inert matter back to pure Spirit. See *God Talks With Arjuna: The Bhagavad Gita,* pages 63 ff., commentary on I:4 – 6. *(Publisher's Note)*

to cooperate with His work of salvation in their lives.

❖ ❖ ❖

It was of that Infinite Consciousness, replete with the love and bliss of God, that Saint John spoke when he said: "As many as received him [the Christ Consciousness], to them gave he power to become the sons of God." Thus according to Jesus' own teaching as recorded by his most highly advanced apostle, John, all souls who become united with Christ Consciousness by intuitive Self-realization are rightly called sons of God.

❖ ❖ ❖

To receive Christ is not accomplished through church membership, nor by outer ritual of acknowledging Jesus as one's savior but never knowing him in reality by contacting him in meditation. To know Christ signifies to close the eyes, expand the consciousness and so deepen the concentration that through the inner light of soul intuition one partakes of the same consciousness that Jesus had.

Saint John and other advanced disciples of Jesus who truly "received him" felt him as the Christ Consciousness present in every speck of space. A true Christian—a Christ-one—is he who frees his soul from the consciousness of the body and unites it with the Christ Intelligence pervading all creation.

❖ ❖ ❖

A small cup cannot hold an ocean within itself. Likewise, the cup of human consciousness, limited by the physical and mental instrumentalities of material perceptions, cannot grasp the universal Christ Consciousness, no matter how desirous one may be of doing so. By the definite science of meditation known for millenniums to the yogis and sages of India, and to Jesus, any seeker of God can enlarge the caliber of his consciousness to omniscience—to receive within himself the Universal Intelligence of God.

❖ ❖ ❖

The divine power of Christ realization is an internal experience; it may be received through unalloyed devotion for God and for His pure reflection as Christ. The power of church and temple will vanish. Real spirituality shall come from the temples of great souls who are day and night in the ecstasy of God. Such souls as I have seen in India surpass the glory of all the temples. Remember, Christ seeks the temples of true souls. He loves the quiet shrine of devotion in your heart where you abide with him, there in the sanctuary aglow with the vigil light of your love. Those who meditate devoutly will receive Christ on the altar of calmness in their own consciousness.

❖ ❖ ❖

In titling this work *The Second Coming of Christ,** I am not referring to a literal return of Jesus to earth. He came two thousand years ago and, after imparting a universal path to God's kingdom, was crucified and resurrected; his reappearance to the masses now is not necessary for the fulfillment of his teachings. What *is* necessary is for the cosmic wisdom and divine perception of Jesus to speak again through each one's own experience and understanding of the infinite Christ Consciousness that was incarnate in Jesus. That will be his true Second Coming.

❖ ❖ ❖

Real Christ followers are those who embrace in their own consciousness through meditation and ecstasy the omnipresent cosmic wisdom and bliss of Jesus Christ....Devotees who want to be real Christ-ians, rather than just members of Christian churchianity, must know and truly feel the presence of Omnipresent Christ all the time, must commune with Him in ecstasy, and be guided by His Infinite Wisdom.

❖ ❖ ❖

These teachings have been sent to explain the truth as Jesus intended it to be known in the world—not to give a new Christianity, but to give the real Christ-teaching: how to become like Christ, how to resurrect the Eternal Christ within one's Self.

---

* I.e., the larger work by Paramahansa Yogananda from which *The Yoga of Jesus* is extracted.

CHAPTER 2

Jesus and Yoga

The continuity of God's word through His avatars [was] beautifully symbolized by the spiritual exchange between Jesus at his birth and the Wise Men of India come to honor his incarnation.

❖ ❖ ❖

There is a very strong tradition in India, authoritatively known amongst high metaphysicians in tales well told and written in ancient manuscripts, that the wise men of the East who made their way to the infant Jesus in Bethlehem were, in fact, great sages of India. Not only did the Indian masters come to Jesus, but he reciprocated their visit.

During the unaccounted-for years of Jesus' life—the Scripture remains silent about him from approximately age fourteen to thirty—he journeyed to India, probably traveling the well-established trade route that linked the Mediterranean with China and India.

His own God-realization, reawakened and reinforced in the company of the masters and the spiritual environs of India, provided a background of the universality of truth from which he could preach a simple, open message comprehensible to the masses of his native country, yet with underlying meanings that would be appreciated in generations to come as the infancy of man's mind would mature in understanding.

The "Lost Years" of Jesus

In the New Testament, the curtain of silence comes down on the life of Jesus after his twelfth year, not to rise once more until eighteen years later, at which time he receives baptism from John and begins preaching to the multitude. We are told only: *"And Jesus increased in wisdom and stature, and in favor with God and man"* (Luke 2:52).

❄ *11* ❦

For the contemporaries of such an extraordinary figure to find nothing noteworthy to record from his childhood to his thirtieth year is in and of itself extraordinary.

Remarkable accounts, however, do exist, not in the land of Jesus' birth but farther east where he spent most of the unaccounted-for years. Hidden away in a Tibetan monastery priceless records lie. They speak of a Saint Issa from Israel "in whom was manifest the soul of the universe";

India: Mother of Religion

A wealth of evidence for the primacy of India's spiritual culture in the ancient world is presented by Georg Feuerstein, Ph.D., Subhash Kak, Ph.D., and David Frawley, O.M.D., in *In Search of the Cradle of Civilization: New Light on Ancient India* (Wheaton, Ill.: Quest Books, 1995): "The old saying *ex oriente lux* ('From the East, light') is no platitude, for civilization's torch, especially the core sacred tradition of perennial wisdom, has been handed down from the eastern hemisphere....The Middle-Eastern creations of Judaism and Christianity, which largely have given our civilization its present shape, were influenced by ideas stemming from countries farther east, especially India."

The scriptures of India "are the oldest extant philosophy and psychology of our race," says renowned historian Will Durant in *Our Oriental Heritage* (*The Story of Civilization,* Part I). Robert C. Priddy, professor of the history of philosophy at the University of Oslo, wrote in *On India's Ancient Past* (1999): "India's past is so ancient and has been so influential in the rise of civilization and religion, at least for almost everyone in the Old World, that most people can claim it actually to be the earliest part of our own odyssey....The mother of religion, the world's earliest spiritual teachings of the Vedic tradition contains the most sublime and allembracing of philosophies."

In his two-volume work *India and World Civilization* (Michigan State University Press, 1969), historian D. P. Singhal amasses abundant documentation of India's spiritual nurturing of the ancient world. He describes the excavation of a vase near Baghdad that has led researchers to the conclusion that "by the middle of the third millennium B.C., an Indian cult was already being practiced in Mesopotamia.... Archaeology has thus shown that two thousand years before the earliest references in cuneiform texts to contact with India, she was sending her manufactures to the land where the roots of Western civilization lie." *(Publisher's Note)*

who from the age of fourteen to twenty-eight was in India and regions of the Himalayas among the saints, monks, and pundits; who preached his message throughout that area and then returned to teach in his native land, where he was treated vilely, condemned, and put to death. Except as chronicled in these ancient manuscripts, no other history of the unknown years of Jesus' life has ever been published.

Providentially, these ancient records were discovered and copied [in the Himis Monastery in Tibet] by a Russian traveler, Nicholas Notovitch....He published his notes himself in 1894 under the title *The Unknown Life of Jesus Christ....*

In 1922, Swami Abhedananda, a direct disciple of Ramakrishna Paramahansa, visited the Himis Monastery, and confirmed all of the salient details about Issa published in Notovitch's book.

Nicholas Roerich, in an expedition to India and Tibet in the mid-1920s, saw and copied verses from ancient manuscripts that were the same, or at least the same in content, as those published by Notovitch. He was also deeply impressed by the oral traditions of that area: "In Srinagar we first encountered the curious legend about Christ's visit to this place. Afterwards we saw how widely spread in India, in Ladak and in Central Asia, was the legend of the visit of Christ to these parts during his long absence, quoted in the Gospel."

❖ ❖ ❖

India is the mother of religion. Her civilization has been acknowledged as much older than the legendary civilization of Egypt. If you study these matters, you will see how the hoary scriptures of India, predating all other revelations, have influenced the Book of the Dead of Egypt and the Old and New Testaments of the Bible, as well as other religions. All were in touch with, and drew from, the religion of India, because India specialized in religion from time immemorial.

So it was that Jesus himself went to India; Notovitch's manuscript tells us: "Issa secretly absented himself from his father's house; left Jerusalem, and, in a train of merchants, journeyed toward the Sindh, with the object of perfecting himself in the knowledge of the Word of God and the study of the laws of the great Buddhas."*

❖ ❖ ❖

This is not to say that Jesus learned everything he taught from his spiritual mentors and associates in India and surrounding regions. Avatars come with their own endowment of wisdom. Jesus' store of divine realization was merely awakened and molded to fit his unique mission by his sojourn among the Hindu pundits, Buddhist monks, and particularly the great masters of yoga from whom he received initiation in the esoteric science of God-union through meditation. From the knowledge he had gleaned, and from the wisdom brought forth from his soul in deep meditation, he distilled for the masses simple parables of the ideal principles by which to govern one's life in the sight of God. But to those close disciples who were ready to receive it, he taught the deeper mysteries, as evidenced in the New Testament book of Revelation of Saint John, the symbology of which accords exactly with the yoga science of God-realization. *[See page 33.]*

❖ ❖ ❖

The documents discovered by Notovitch lend historical support to my long-held assertion, gleaned from my earliest years in India, that Jesus was linked with the *rishis* of India through the Wise Men who journeyed to his cradle, and for whom he went to India to receive their blessings and to confer concerning his world mission. That his teaching, born internally from his God-realization and nurtured externally by his studies with the masters, expresses the universality of Christ Consciousness that knows no boundary of race or creed, is what I shall endeavor to make evident throughout the pages of this book.

Like the sun, which rises in the East and travels to the West spreading its rays, so Christ rose in the East and came to the West, there to be enshrined in a vast Christendom whose adherents look to him as their guru and savior. It is no happenstance that Jesus chose to be born an Oriental

---

* Cf. Swami Abhedananda's translation of this verse from the Tibetan: "At this time his great desire was to achieve full realisation of godhead and learn religion at the feet of those who have attained perfection through meditation." —*Journey into Kashmir and Tibet*

Christ in Palestine. This locale was the hub linking the East with Europe. He traveled to India to honor his ties with her *rishis*, preached his message throughout that area, and then went back to spread his teachings in Palestine, which he saw in his great wisdom as the doorway through which his spirit and words would find their way to Europe and the rest of the world. This great Christ, radiating the spiritual strength and power of the Orient to the West, is a divine liaison to unite God-loving peoples of East and West.

Truth is not the monopoly of the Orient or the Occident. The pure silver-gold rays of sunlight appear to be red or blue when observed through red or blue glass. So, also, truth only appears to be different when colored by an Oriental or Occidental civilization. In looking at the simple essence of truth expressed by the great ones of various times and climes, one finds very little difference in their messages. What I received from my Guru and the venerated masters of India I find the same as that which I have received from the teachings of Jesus the Christ.

The Lost Teachings of the Gospels

Christ has been much misinterpreted by the world. Even the most elementary principles of his teachings have been desecrated, and their esoteric depths have been forgotten. They have been crucified at the hands of dogma, prejudice, and cramped understanding. Genocidal wars have been fought, people have been burned as witches and heretics, on the presumed authority of man-made doctrines of Christianity. How to salvage the immortal teachings from the hands of ignorance? We must know Jesus as an Oriental Christ, a supreme yogi who manifested full mastery of the universal science of God-union, and thus could speak and act as a savior with the voice and authority of God. He has been Westernized too much.

Jesus was an Oriental, by birth and blood and training. To separate a teacher from the background of his nationality is to blur the understanding through which he is perceived. No matter what Jesus the Christ was himself, as regards his own soul, being born and maturing in the Orient, he had to use the medium of Oriental civilization, customs, mannerisms, language, parables, in spreading his message. Hence to understand Jesus

Gnostic Gospels: The Lost Christianity?

Through the remarkable discovery of early Christian gnostic texts at Nag Hammadi, Egypt, in 1945, one may glimpse something of what was lost to conventional Christianity during this process of "Westernization." Elaine Pagels, Ph.D., writes in *The Gnostic Gospels* (New York: Vintage Books, 1981):

"The Nag Hammadi texts, and others like them, which circulated at the beginning of the Christian era, were denounced as heresy by orthodox Christians in the middle of the second century....But those who wrote and circulated these texts did not regard *themselves* as 'heretics.' Most of the writings use Christian terminology, unmistakably related to a Jewish heritage. Many claim to offer traditions about Jesus that are secret, hidden from 'the many' who constitute what, in the second century, came to be called the 'catholic church.' These Christians are now called gnostics, from the Greek word *gnosis,* usually translated as 'knowledge.' For as those who claim to know nothing about ultimate reality are called agnostic (literally, 'not-knowing'), the person who does claim to know such things is called gnostic ('knowing'). But *gnosis* is not primarily rational knowledge....As the gnostics use the term, we could translate it as 'insight,' for *gnosis* involves an intuitive process of knowing oneself....[According to gnostic teachers,] to know oneself, at the deepest level, is simultaneously to know God; this is the secret of *gnosis....*

"The 'living Jesus' of these texts speaks of illusion and enlightenment, not of sin and repentance, like the Jesus of the New Testament. Instead of coming to save us from sin, he comes as a guide who opens access to spiritual understanding....

"Orthodox Christians believe that Jesus is Lord and Son of God in a unique way: he remains forever distinct from the rest of humanity whom he came to save. Yet the gnostic *Gospel of Thomas* relates that as soon as Thomas recognizes him, Jesus says to Thomas that they have both received their being from the same source: 'I am not your master. Because you have drunk, you have become drunk from the bubbling stream which I have measured out....He who will drink from my mouth will become as I am: I myself shall become he, and the things that are hidden will be revealed to him.'

"Does not such teaching—the identity of the divine and human, the concern with illusion and enlightenment, the founder who is presented not as Lord, but as spiritual guide—sound more Eastern than Western?...Could Hindu or Buddhist traditions have influenced gnosticism?....Ideas that we associate with Eastern religions emerged in the first century through the gnostic movement in the West, but they were suppressed and condemned by polemicists like Irenaeus." *(Publisher's Note)*

Christ and his teachings one must be sympathetically open to the Oriental point of view—in particular, India's ancient and present civilization, religious scriptures, traditions, philosophies, spiritual beliefs, and intuitive metaphysical experiences. Though, esoterically understood, the teachings of Jesus are universal, they are saturated with the essence of Oriental culture—rooted in Oriental influences which have been made adaptable to the Western environment.

The Gospels can be rightly understood in the light of the teachings of India—not the caste-ridden, stone-worshiping, distorted interpretations of Hinduism, but the philosophical, soul-saving wisdom of her *rishis:* the kernel not the husk of the Vedas, Upanishads, and Bhagavad Gita. This essence of Truth—the *Sanatana Dharma,* or eternal principles of righteousness that uphold man and the universe—was given to the world thousands of years before the Christian era, and preserved in India with a spiritual vitality that has made the quest for God the be-all and end-all of life and not an armchair diversion.

The Universal Science of Religion

The personal realization of truth is the science behind all sciences. But for most persons, religion has devolved to a matter of belief only. One believes in Catholicism, another believes in some Protestant denomination, others assert belief that the Jewish or Hindu or Muslim or Buddhist religion is the true way. The science of religion identifies the universal truths common to all—the basis of religion—and teaches how by their practical application persons can build their lives according to the Divine Plan. India's teaching of *Raja Yoga,* the "royal" science of the soul, supersedes the orthodoxy of religion by setting forth systematically the practice of those methods that are universally necessary for the perfection of every individual, regardless of race or creed.

❖ ❖ ❖

What is needed is a reunion of the science of religion with the spirit, or inspiration, of religion—the esoteric with the exoteric. The yoga science taught by Lord Krishna, which provides practical methods for actual inner experience of God to supplant the feeble life-expectancy of beliefs, and the spirit of Christ-love and brotherhood preached by Jesus—the only sure panacea to prevent the world from tearing itself apart by its unyielding differences—are in tandem one and the same universal truth, taught by these two Christs of East and West.

❖ ❖ ❖

The saviors of the world do not come to foster inimical doctrinal divisions; their teachings should not be used toward that end. It is something of a misnomer even to refer to the New Testament as the "Christian" Bible, for it does not belong exclusively to any one sect. Truth is meant for the blessing and upliftment of the entire human race. As the Christ Consciousness is universal, so does Jesus Christ belong to all.

Though I emphasize the message of Lord Jesus in the New Testament and the yoga science of God-union delineated by Bhagavan Krishna in the Bhagavad Gita as the *summum bonum* of the way to God-realization, I honor the diverse expressions of truth flowing from the One God through the scriptures of His various emissaries.

❖ ❖ ❖

Truth, in and of itself, is the ultimate "religion." Though truth can be expressed in different ways by sectarian "isms," it can never be exhausted by them. It has infinite manifestations and ramifications, but one consummation: direct experience of God, the Sole Reality.

The human stamp of sectarian affiliation is of little meaning. It is not the religious denomination in which one's name is registered, nor the culture or creed in which one was born, that gives salvation. The essence of truth goes beyond all outer form. It is that essence which is paramount in understanding Jesus and his universal call to souls to enter the kingdom of God, which is "within you."

❖ ❖ ❖

We are all children of God, from our inception unto eternity. Differences come from prejudices, and prejudice is the child of ignorance. We should not proudly identify ourselves as Americans or Indians or Italians or any other nationality, for that is but an accident of birth. Above all else, we should be proud that we are children of God, made in His image. Is not that the message of Christ?

Jesus the Christ is an excellent model for both East and West to follow. God's stamp, "son of God," is hidden in every soul. Jesus affirmed the scriptures: "Ye are gods."

Do away with masks! Come out openly as sons of God—not by hollow proclamations and learned-by-heart prayers, fireworks of intellectually worded sermons contrived to praise God and gather converts, but by *realization*! Become identified not with narrow bigotry, masked as wisdom, but with Christ Consciousness. Become identified with Universal Love, expressed in service to all, both materially and spiritually; then you will know who Jesus Christ was, and can say in your soul that we are all one band, all sons of One God!

"I like your teachings. But are you a Christian?" The questioner was talking for the first time with Paramahansaji. The Guru replied:

"Didn't Christ tell us: 'Not every one that saith unto me, Lord, Lord, shall enter into the kingdom of heaven; but he that doeth the will of my Father which is in heaven'?

"In the Bible the term heathen *means an idolater: one whose attention is centered not on the Lord but on the attractions of the world. A materialist may go to church on Sundays and still be a heathen. He who keeps ever alight the lamp of remembrance of the Heavenly Father and who obeys the precepts of Jesus is a Christian."*

He added, *"It is for you to decide whether or not you think I am a Christian."*

—Sayings of Paramahansa Yogananda

CHAPTER 3

Inner Teachings of Jesus the Yogi
How Every Soul Can Attain Christ Consciousness

The Importance of the Comforter, or Holy Ghost

"If ye love me keep my commandments. And I will pray the Father, and He shall give you another Comforter, that He may abide with you for ever; even the Spirit of truth; whom the world cannot receive, because it seeth Him not, neither knoweth Him: but ye know Him; for He dwelleth with you, and shall be in you. I will not leave you comfortless....

"But the Comforter, which is the Holy Ghost, whom the Father will send in my name, he shall teach you all things, and bring all things to your remembrance, whatsoever I have said unto you.

"Peace I leave with you, my peace I give unto you: not as the world giveth, give I unto you. Let not your heart be troubled, neither let it be afraid" (John 14:15 – 18, 26, 27).

Today the same admonition applies that Jesus gave to his immediate disciples. If a devotee loves him (that is, loves contact with the Christ Consciousness in him) then he or she must faithfully follow the commandments—the laws of bodily and mental discipline and meditation—which are required to manifest the Christ Consciousness in the individual's own consciousness.

❖ ❖ ❖

The promise of Jesus to send the Holy Ghost after he was gone few in the Christian world have understood. Holy Ghost is the sacred, invisible vibratory power of God that actively sustains the universe: the Word, or *Aum,* Cosmic Vibration, the Great Comforter, the Savior from all sorrows.

The Word: God's Intelligent Cosmic Vibration

The scientific evolution of cosmic creation from the Creator-Lord is outlined, in arcane terminology, in the Old Testament book of Genesis. In the New Testament, the opening verses of Saint John's Gospel may rightly be called Genesis According to Saint John. Both these profound Biblical accounts, when clearly grasped by intuitive perception, correspond exactly to the spiritual cosmology set forth in the scriptures of India handed down by her Golden Age God-knowing *rishis*.

Saint John was perhaps the greatest of the disciples of Jesus. Just as a schoolteacher finds among his pupils one whose superior comprehension ranks him first in the class, and others who must be ranked lower, so among the disciples of Jesus there were differing degrees of ability

The "Word" in Original Christianity

Though official church doctrine for centuries has interpreted "the Word" (*Logos* in the original Greek) to be a reference to Jesus himself, that was not the understanding originally intended by Saint John in this passage. According to scholars, the concept John was expressing can best be understood not through the exegesis of much-later church orthodoxy, but through the scriptural writings and the teachings of Jewish philosophers of John's own period—for example, the Book of Proverbs (with which John and any other Jewish person of his time would have been familiar). Karen Armstrong in *A History of God: The 4,000 Year Quest of Judaism, Christianity, and Islam* (New York: Alfred A. Knopf, 1993) writes: "The author of the Book of Proverbs, who was writing in the third century BCE...personifies Wisdom so that she seems a separate person:

"Yahweh created me [Wisdom] when his purpose first unfolded, before the oldest of his works. From everlasting I was firmly set, from the beginning, before earth came into being...when he laid the foundations of the earth, I was at his side, a master craftsman, delighting him day after day, ever at play in his presence, at play everywhere in the world, delighting to be with the sons of men" (Proverbs 8:22–23, 30–31; The Jerusalem Bible)....

"In the Aramaic translations of the Hebrew scriptures known as the *targums*, which were being composed at this time [i.e., when the John's Gospel was written], the term *Memra* (word) is used to describe God's activity in the world. It performs

to appreciate and absorb the depth and breadth of the teachings of the Christ-man. The records left by Saint John, among the various books of the New Testament, evince the highest degree of divine realization, making known the deep esoteric truths experienced by Jesus and transferred to John. Not only in his gospel, but in his epistles and especially in the profound metaphysical experiences symbolically described in the Book of Revelation, John presents the truths taught by Jesus from the point of view of inward intuitive realization. In John's words we find precision; that is why his gospel, though last among the four in the New Testament, should be considered first when the true meaning of the life and teachings of Jesus is being sought.

❖ ❖ ❖

the same function as other technical terms like 'glory,' 'Holy Spirit,' and 'Shekinah' which emphasized the distinction between God's presence in the world and the incomprehensible reality of God itself. Like the divine Wisdom, the 'Word' symbolized God's original plan for creation."

The writings of early Church Fathers also indicate that this was the meaning intended by Saint John. In *Clement of Alexandria* (Edinburgh: William Blackwood and Sons, 1914) John Patrick states: "Clement repeatedly identifies the Word with the Wisdom of God." And Dr. Anne Pasquier, professor of theology at Université Laval, Quebec, writes in *The Nag Hammadi Library After Fifty Years* (John D. Turner and Anne McGuire, editors; New York: Brill, 1997): "Philo, Clement of Alexandria, and Origen...all associate the Logos with the word of God in the Old Testament accounts of the creation when 'God spoke and it was done.' The Valentinians do likewise....According to the Valentinians, the prologue to John's Gospel depicts a spiritual genesis, the model for the material one, and it is seen as a spiritual interpretation of the Old Testament accounts of the creation."

However, the "Word" (as also "the only begotten Son") came to signify the *person* of Jesus only through a gradual evolution of doctrine brought about by complex theological and political influences. It was not until the fourth century, writes historian Karen Armstrong in *A History of God,* that the church came to "adopt an exclusive notion of religious truth: Jesus was the first and last Word of God to the human race." *(Publisher's Note)*

"In the beginning...." With these words commence the cosmogonies of the Old and New Testament alike. "Beginning" refers to the birth of finite creation, for in the Eternal Absolute—Spirit—there is neither beginning nor end....

Spirit, being the only existing Substance, had naught but Itself with which to create. Spirit and Its universal creation could not be essentially different, for two ever-existing Infinite Forces would consequently each be absolute, which is by definition an impossibility. An orderly creation requires the duality of Creator and created. Thus, Spirit first gave rise to a Magic Delusion, Maya, the cosmic Magical Measurer,* which produces the illusion of dividing a portion of the Indivisible Infinite into separate finite objects, even as a calm ocean becomes distorted into individual waves on its surface by the action of a storm.

All creation is nothing but Spirit, seemingly and temporarily diversified by Spirit's creative vibratory activity.

❖ ❖ ❖

In the beginning was the Word, and the Word was with God, and the Word was God. The same was in the beginning with God.

All things were made by him; and without him was not any thing made that was made.

In him was life; and the life was the light of men (John 1:1–4).

"Word" means intelligent vibration, intelligent energy, going forth from God. Any utterance of a word, such as "flower," expressed by an intelligent being, consists of sound energy or vibration, plus thought, which imbues that vibration with intelligent meaning. Likewise, the Word that is the beginning and source of all created substances is Cosmic Vibration [Holy Ghost] imbued with Cosmic Intelligence [Christ Consciousness].

Thought of matter, energy of which matter is composed, matter itself—all things—are but the differently vibrating thoughts of the Spirit.

❖ ❖ ❖

---

* The Sanskrit word *maya* (cosmic delusion) means "the measurer"; it is the magical power in creation by which limitations and divisions are apparently present in the Immeasurable and Inseparable.

Before creation, there is only undifferentiated Spirit. In manifesting creation, Spirit becomes God the Father, Son, and Holy Ghost....

The Unmanifested Spirit became God the Father, the Creator of all creative vibration. God the Father, in the Hindu scriptures, is called *Ishvara* (the Cosmic Ruler) or *Sat* (the supreme pure essence of Cosmic Consciousness)—the Transcendental Intelligence. That is, God the Father exists transcendentally untouched by any tremor of vibratory creation—a conscious, separate Cosmic Consciousness.

The vibratory force emanating from Spirit, endowed with the illusory creative power of *maya*, is the Holy Ghost: Cosmic Vibration, the Word, *Aum (Om)* or Amen.

❖ ❖ ❖

The Word, the creative energy and sound of Cosmic Vibration, like the sound waves of an unimaginably powerful earthquake, went out of the Creator to manifest the universe. That Cosmic Vibration, permeated with Cosmic Intelligence, was condensed into subtle elements—thermal, electric, magnetic, and all manner of rays; thence into atoms of vapor (gases), liquids, and solids.

❖ ❖ ❖

A cosmic vibration omnipresently active in space could not of itself create or sustain the wondrously complex cosmos....[Thus] the transcendent consciousness of God the Father became manifest within the Holy Ghost vibration as the Son—the Christ Consciousness, God's intelligence in all vibratory creation. This pure reflection of God in the Holy Ghost indirectly guides it to create, re-create, preserve, and mold creation according to God's divine purpose.

❖ ❖ ❖

The Biblical writers, not versed in the terminologies that express the knowledge of the modern age, quite aptly used "Holy Ghost" and "the Word" to designate the character of the Intelligent Cosmic Vibration. "Word" implies a vibratory sound, carrying materializing power. "Ghost" implies an intelligent, invisible, conscious force. "Holy" describes this Vibration because it is the manifestation of Spirit; and because it is trying to create the universe according to the perfect pattern of God.

The Vibratory Nature of Creation

Recent advances in what theoretical physicists call "superstring theory" are leading science toward an understanding of the vibratory nature of creation. Brian Greene, Ph.D., professor of physics at Cornell and Columbia Universities, writes in *The Elegant Universe: Superstrings, Hidden Dimensions, and the Quest for the Ultimate Theory* (New York: Vintage Books, 2000):

"During the last thirty years of his life, Albert Einstein sought relentlessly for a so-called unified field theory—a theory capable of describing nature's forces within a single, all-encompassing, coherent framework....Now, at the dawn of the new millennium, proponents of string theory claim that the threads of this elusive unified tapestry finally have been revealed....

"The theory suggests that the microscopic landscape is suffused with tiny strings whose vibrational patterns orchestrate the evolution of the universe," Professor Greene writes, and tells us that "the length of a typical string loop is...about a hundred billion billion (10^{20}) times smaller than an atomic nucleus."

Professor Greene explains that by the end of the twentieth century, science had determined that the physical universe was composed of a very few fundamental particles, such as electrons, quarks (which are the building blocks of protons and neutrons), and neutrinos. "Although each particle was viewed as elementary," he writes, "the kind of 'stuff' each embodied was thought to be different. Electron 'stuff,' for example, had negative electric charge, while neutrino 'stuff' had no electric charge. String theory alters this picture radically by declaring that the 'stuff' of all matter and all forces is the *same*."

"According to string theory, there is only *one* fundamental ingredient—the string," Greene writes in *The Fabric of the Cosmos: Space, Time, and the Texture of Reality* (New York: Alfred A. Knopf, 2004). He explains that "just as a violin string can vibrate in different patterns, each of which produces a distinct musical tone, the filaments of superstring theory can also vibrate in different patterns....A tiny string vibrating in one pattern would have the mass and the electric charge of an electron; according to the theory, such a vibrating string would *be* what we have traditionally called an electron. A tiny string vibrating in a different pattern would have the requisite properties to identify it as a quark, a neutrino, or any other kind of particle....Each arises from a different vibrational pattern executed by the same underlying entity....At the ultramicroscopic level, the universe would be akin to a string symphony vibrating matter into existence." *(Publisher's Note)*

The designation in the Hindu scriptures of this "Holy Ghost" as *Aum* signifies its role in God's creative plan: *A* stands for *akara,* or creative vibration; *u* for *ukara,* preservative vibration; and *m* for *makara,* the vibratory power of dissolution. A storm roaring across the sea creates waves, large and small, preserves them for some time, and then by withdrawing dissolves them. So the *Aum* or Holy Ghost creates all things, preserves them in myriad forms, and ultimately dissolves them in the sea-bosom of God to be again re-created—a continuing process of renewal of life and form in the ongoing cosmic dreaming of God.

Thus is the Word or Cosmic Vibration the origin of "all things": "without him was not anything made that was made." The Word existed from the very beginning of creation—God's first manifestation in bringing forth the universe. "The Word was with God"—imbued with God's reflected intelligence, Christ Consciousness—"and the Word was God"—vibrations of His own one Being.

Saint John's declaration echoes an eternal truth resonating in various passages of the hoary Vedas: that the cosmic vibratory Word (*Vak*) was with God the Father-Creator (*Prajapati*) in the beginning of creation, when naught else existed; and that by *Vak* were made all things; and that *Vak* is itself Brahman (God).

❖ ❖ ❖

"These things saith the Amen [the Word, *Aum*], the faithful and true witness, the beginning of the creation of God."* The holy Cosmic Sound of *Aum* or Amen is the witness of the manifested Divine Presence in all creation.

Father, Son, and Holy Ghost According to Yoga

The Holy Trinity of Christianity—Father, Son, and Holy Ghost—in relation to the ordinary concept of the incarnation of Jesus is wholly inexplicable without differentiating between Jesus the body and Jesus

---

* Revelation 3:14. *Aum* of the Vedas became the sacred word *Hum* of the Tibetans, *Amin* of the Moslems, and *Amen* of the Egyptians, Greeks, Romans, Jews, and Christians. The meaning of *Amen* in Hebrew is "sure, faithful."

the vehicle in which the only begotten Son, Christ Consciousness, was manifested. Jesus himself makes such distinction when speaking of his body as the "son of man"; and of his soul, which was not circumscribed by the body but was one with the only begotten Christ Consciousness in all specks of vibration, as the "son of God."

"God so loved the world, that He gave His only begotten Son" to redeem it; that is, God the Father remained hidden beyond the vibratory realm that went out from His Being, but then secreted Himself as the Christ Intelligence in all matter and in all living beings in order to bring, by beautiful evolutional coaxings, all things back to His home of Everlasting Blessedness. Without this presence of God ubiquitously permeating creation, man would indeed feel bereft of Divine Succor—how sweetly, sometimes almost imperceptibly, It comes to his aid when he bows his knee in supplication. His Creator and Supreme Benefactor is never more than a devotional thought away.

Saint John said: "As many as received him, to them gave he power to become the sons of God." The plural number in "sons of God" shows distinctly, from the teachings he received from Jesus, that not the body of Jesus but his state of Christ Consciousness was the only begotten son; and that all those who could clarify their consciousness and receive, or in an unobstructed way reflect, the power of God, could become the sons of God. They could be one with the only begotten reflection of God in all matter, as was Jesus; and through the son, Christ Consciousness, ascend to the Father, the supreme Cosmic Consciousness.

❖ ❖ ❖

India's priceless contribution to the world, discovered anciently by her *rishis,* is the science of religion—yoga, "divine union"—by which God can be known, not as a theological concept but as an actual personal experience. Of all scientific knowledge, the yoga science of God-realization is of the highest value to man, for it strikes at the root-cause of all human maladies: ignorance, the beclouding envelopment of delusion. When one becomes firmly established in God-realization, delusion is transcended and the subordinate mortal consciousness is elevated to Christlike status.

Receiving Christ Consciousness by Communion With the Holy Ghost in Meditation

But as many as received him, to them gave he power to become the sons of God, even to them that believe on his name: Which were born, not of blood, nor of the will of the flesh, nor of the will of man, but of God (John 1:12–13).

The light of God shines equally in all, but because of delusive ignorance all do not receive, reflect, it alike. Sunlight falls the same on a lump of coal and a diamond, but only the diamond receives and reflects the light in brilliant splendor. The carbon in the coal has the potential to become a diamond. All it requires is conversion under high pressure. So it is said here that everyone can be like Christ—whosoever clarifies his consciousness by a moral and spiritual life, and especially by the purification of meditation in which rudimentary mortality is sublimed into the soul's perfection of immortality.

To be a son of God is not something one has to acquire: rather, one has only to receive His light and realize God has already conferred on him, at his very inception, that blessed status.

"Even to them that believe on his name": When even the Name of God rouses one's devotion and anchors one's thoughts in Him, it becomes a door to salvation. When the mere mention of His name sets the soul afire with love for God, it will start the devotee on his way to liberation.

The deeper meaning of "name" is a reference to Cosmic Vibration (the Word, *Aum*, Amen). God as Spirit has no circumscribing name. Whether one refers to the Absolute as God or Jehovah or Brahman or Allah, that does not express Him. God the Creator and Father of all vibrates through nature as the eternal life, and that life has the sound of the great Amen or *Aum*. That name most accurately defines God. "Those who believe on his name" means those who commune with that *Aum* sound, the voice of God in the Holy Ghost vibration. When one hears that name of God, that Cosmic Vibration, he is on his way to becoming a son of God, for in that sound his consciousness touches the immanent Christ Consciousness, which will introduce him to God as Cosmic Consciousness.

Sage Patanjali, India's greatest exponent of yoga, describes God the Creator as Ishvara, the Cosmic Lord or Ruler. "His symbol is *Pranava* (the Holy Word or Sound, *Aum*). By prayerful, repeated chanting of *Aum* and meditation on its meaning, obstacles disappear and the consciousness turns inward (away from external sensory identification)" (*Yoga Sutras* I:27–29).*

❖ ❖ ❖

Essential sons of God, clear reflections of the Father untarnished by delusion, have become sons of man by identification with the flesh and forgetfulness of their origin in Spirit. Deluded man is just a beggar on the street of time. But as Jesus received and reflected through his purified consciousness the divine sonship of Christ Consciousness, so also every man, by yoga meditation, can clarify his mind and become a diamond-like mentality who will receive and reflect the light of God.

❖ ❖ ❖

The method of contacting this Cosmic Vibration, the Holy Ghost, is for the first time being spread worldwide by means of definite meditation techniques of the *Kriya Yoga* science. Through the blessing of communion with the Holy Ghost, the cup of human consciousness is expanded to receive the ocean of Christ Consciousness. The adept in the practice of the science of *Kriya Yoga* who consciously experiences the presence of the Holy Ghost Comforter and merges in the Son, or immanent Christ Consciousness, attains thereby realization of God the Father and entry into the infinite kingdom of God.

Christ will thus appear a second time in the consciousness of every devout adept who masters the technique of contacting the Holy Ghost, the bestower of indescribable blissful comfort in Spirit.

* Patanjali's date is unknown, though many scholars assign him to the second century B.C. His renowned *Yoga Sutras* presents, in a series of brief aphorisms, the condensed essence of the exceedingly vast and intricate science of God-union—setting forth the method of uniting the soul with the undifferentiated Spirit in such a beautiful, clear, and concise way that generations of scholars have acknowledged the *Yoga Sutras* as the foremost ancient work on yoga.

Baptism by the Holy Ghost

The ultimate baptism, acclaimed by John the Baptist and by all Self-realized masters, is to be baptized "with the Holy Ghost, and with fire" — that is, to become permeated with God's presence in the holy Creative Vibration whose omnipresent omniscience not only uplifts and expands the consciousness, but whose fire of cosmic life energy actually cauterizes sins of present bad habits and karmic effects of past erroneous actions.

❖ ❖ ❖

The uplifting vibrations of "the Comforter" bring profound inner peace and joy. The Creative Vibration vitalizes the individual life force in the body, which conduces to health and well-being, and can be consciously directed as healing power to those in need of divine aid. Being the source of intelligent creativity, the *Aum* vibration inspires one's own initiative, ingenuity, and will.

❖ ❖ ❖

By contacting God…in meditation, all desires of the heart are fulfilled; for nothing is more worthwhile, more pleasant or attractive than the all-satisfying, ever-new joy of God….One who bathes his consciousness in the Holy Ghost becomes unattached to personal desires and objects while enjoying everything with the joyousness of God within.

❖ ❖ ❖

[An ecstatic experience of Paramahansa Yogananda in communion with the Holy Ghost Cosmic Vibration of Aum:]

"When sensory perceptions vibrate their pleasures in the body, I experience a heaviness; a weighty load hangs on the bosom of my soul, and I feel drawn down to matter. But, O elevating *Aum*, when Thou dost vibrate within me, oh, what exultant joy and lightness I feel. I soar above the body. I am drawn toward Spirit. O great *Aum*, rolling ocean of *Aum*, vibrate long within me so that I may remain awake to Thine infinite presence, broadened into identity with the Universal Spirit. Oh, this is the Voice of Heaven. This is the voice of Spirit. *Aum*, Thou art the source of all life, of all expressions of creation in the universe. So let me feel Thee, O great Mother Vibration, rolling within me as a part of Thy Cosmic Self. Receive me; make me one with Thee. Never leave me; be always rolling within me like a mighty spiritual ocean, calling to me and revealing Thine oceanic presence. O Mighty Vibration, O Mighty Truth that percolates through every atom of my flesh, peace and harmony eternal, bliss and wisdom eternal, come with Thy presence, with Thy universal resonance! Oh, these tiny joys, these tiny tonics of sensual vibrations, I wish to forsake. Enfold me in Thy vibration and carry me along with Thy rolling sound. Let me be free from the bondage of flesh; let me roll on with Thine infinite vibratory ripples of omniscient joy, O great *Aum*. Be with me, possess me, absolve me in Thee."

Yoga Science of the Spine: "Make Straight the Way of the Lord"

There is a beautiful revelation of the way to that divine contact hidden in the Biblical verses where John the Baptist describes himself:

I am the voice of one crying in the wilderness, Make straight the way of the Lord, as said the prophet Isaiah (John 1:23).

When one's senses are engaged outwardly, one is engrossed in the busy mart of creation's interacting complexities of matter. Even when one's eyes are closed in prayer or in other concentrated thoughts, still one is in the domain of busyness. The real wilderness, where no mortal thoughts, restlessness, or human desires, intrude, is in transcendence of the sensory mind, the subconscious mind, and the superconscious mind—in the cosmic consciousness of Spirit, the uncreate trackless "wilderness" of Infinite Bliss.

❖ ❖ ❖

As John heard within himself in the wilderness of silence the all-knowing Cosmic Sound, the intuitive wisdom commanded him silently: "Make straight the way of the Lord." Manifest the Lord, the subjective Christ Consciousness in all cosmic vibratory creation, within yourself through the intuitive feeling awakened when in the state of transcendental ecstasy the divine metaphysical centers of life and consciousness are opened in the straight spinal pathway.

❖ ❖ ❖

Man's body, unique among all creatures, possesses spiritual cerebrospinal centers of divine consciousness in which the descended Spirit is templed. These are known to the yogis, and to Saint John—who described them in Revelation as the seven seals, and as seven stars and seven churches, with their seven angels and seven golden candlesticks.

❖ ❖ ❖

Yoga treatises explain the awakening of the spinal centers not as some mystical aberration but as a purely natural occurrence common to all devotees who find their way into the presence of God. The principles of yoga know no artificial boundaries of religious isms. Yoga is the universal science of divine union of the soul with Spirit, of man with his Maker.

Yoga describes the definite way Spirit descends from Cosmic Consciousness into matter and individualized expression in all beings; and how, conversely, individualized consciousness ultimately must reascend to Spirit.

Yoga and The Book of Revelation

"Write the things which thou hast seen, and the things which are, and the things which shall be hereafter; the mystery of the seven stars which thou sawest in my right hand, and the seven golden candlesticks. The seven stars are the angels of the seven churches: and the seven candlesticks which thou sawest are the seven churches" (Revelation 1:19 – 20).

"And I saw in the right hand of him that sat on the throne a book written within and on the backside, sealed with seven seals. And I saw a strong angel proclaiming with a loud voice, 'Who is worthy to open the book, and to loose the seals thereof?'" (Revelation 5:1 – 2).

Yoga treatises identify these centers (in ascending order) as:

1) *muladhara* (the coccygeal, at the base of the spine);
2) *svadhisthana* (the sacral, two inches above *muladhara*);
3) *manipura* (the lumbar, opposite the navel);
4) *anahata* (the dorsal, opposite the heart);
5) *vishuddha* (the cervical, at the base of the neck);
6) *ajna* (seat of the spiritual eye, traditionally located between the eyebrows; in actuality, directly connected by polarity with the medulla oblongata);
7) *sahasrara* ("thousand-petalled lotus" in the uppermost part of the cerebrum).

The seven centers are divinely planned exits or "trap doors" through which the soul has descended into the body and through which it must reascend by a process of meditation. By seven successive steps, the soul escapes into Cosmic Consciousness. Yoga treatises generally refer to the six lower centers as *chakras* ("wheels," because the concentrated energy in each one is like a hub from which radiate rays of life-giving light and energy), with *sahasrara* referred to separately as a seventh center. All seven centers, however, are often referred to as lotuses, whose petals open, or turn upward, in spiritual awakening as the life and consciousness travel up the spine.

Many are the pathways of religion and the modes of approaching God; but ultimately they all lead to one highway of final ascension to union with Him. The way of liberation of the soul from its ties to mortal consciousness in the body is identical for all: through the same "straight" highway of the spine by which the soul descended from Spirit into the body and matter.*

Man's true nature is the soul, a ray of Spirit. As God is ever-existing, ever-conscious, ever-new Bliss, so the soul, by encasement in the body, is

* "And an highway shall be there, and a way, and it shall be called The way of holiness; the unclean shall not pass over it....but the redeemed shall walk there. And the ransomed of the Lord shall return, and come to Zion with songs and everlasting joy upon their heads: they shall obtain joy and gladness, and sorrow and sighing shall flee away" (Isaiah 35:8–10).

The Astral Body of Life Energy

Scientific discovery of the electromagnetic energy that forms an organizing template for the physical body is described in *Vibrational Medicine* (Rochester, Vermont: Bear and Company, 2001), by Richard Gerber, M.D.: "Neuroanatomist Harold S. Burr at Yale University during the 1940s was studying the shape of energy fields" — which he termed "fields of life" or "L-fields" — "around living plants and animals. Some of Burr's work involved the shape of electrical fields surrounding salamanders. He found that the salamanders possessed an energy field roughly shaped like the adult animal. He also discovered that this field contained an electrical axis which was aligned with the brain and spinal cord. Burr wanted to find precisely when this electrical axis first originated in the animal's development. He began mapping the fields in progressively earlier stages of salamander embryogenesis. Burr discovered that the electrical axis originated in the unfertilized egg.... Burr also experimented with the electrical fields around tiny seedlings. According to his research, the electrical field around a sprout was not the shape of the original seed. Instead the surrounding electrical field resembled the adult plant."

In *Blueprint for Immortality: The Electric Patterns of Life* (Essex, England: Saffron Walden, 1972), Professor Burr describes his research: "Most people who have taken high-school science will remember that if iron filings are scattered on a card held over a magnet they will arrange themselves in the pattern of the 'lines of force'

individualized ever-existing, ever-conscious, ever-new Bliss.

The bodily covering of the soul is threefold in nature. The physical body, with which man so affectionately and tenaciously identifies himself, is little more than inert matter, a clod of earthly minerals and chemicals made up of gross atoms. The physical body receives all its enlivening energy and powers from an inner radiant astral body of lifetrons. The astral body, in turn, is empowered by a causal body of pure consciousness, consisting of all of the ideational principles that structure and maintain the astral and physical bodily instruments employed by the soul to interact with God's creation.

The three bodies are tied together and work as one by a knotting of life force and consciousness in seven spiritual cerebrospinal centers:

of the magnet's field. And if the filings are thrown away and fresh ones scattered on the card, the new filings will assume the same pattern as the old.

"Something like this—though infinitely more complicated—happens in the human body. Its molecules and cells are constantly being torn apart and rebuilt with fresh material from the food we eat. But thanks to the controlling L-field, the new molecules and cells are rebuilt and arrange themselves in the same pattern as the old ones.

"Modern research with 'tagged' elements has revealed that the materials of our bodies and brains are renewed much more often than was previously realized. All the protein in the body, for example, is 'turned over' every six months and, in some organs such as the liver, the protein is renewed much more frequently. When we meet a friend we have not seen for six months there is not one molecule in his face which was there when we last saw him. But, thanks to his controlling L-field, the new molecules have fallen into the old, familiar pattern and we can recognize his face. Until modern instruments revealed the existence of the controlling L-fields, biologists were at a loss to explain how our bodies 'kept in shape' through ceaseless metabolism and changes of material. Now the mystery has been solved, the electrodynamic field of the body serves as a matrix or mould, which preserves the 'shape' or arrangement of any material poured into it, however often the material may be changed." *(Publisher's Note)*

a physical bodily instrument, empowered by the life force of the astral body and the consciousness from the causal form. In its residency in the triune body, the soul takes on the limitations of confinement and becomes the pseudosoul, or ego.

Descending first into the causal body of consciousness through the ideational centers of the causal spine of magnetized consciousness, thence into the wondrous spinal centers of light and power of the astral body, life force and consciousness then descend into the physical body through the brain and spine outward into the nervous system and organs and senses, enabling man to cognize the world and interact with his material environment.

The flow of the life force and consciousness outward through the spine and nerves causes man to perceive and appreciate sensory phenomena only. As attention is the conductor of man's life currents and consciousness, persons who indulge the senses of touch, smell, taste, sound, and sight find the searchlights of their life force and consciousness concentrated on matter.

But when, by self-mastery in meditation, the attention is focused steadily on the center of divine perception at the point between the eyebrows, the searchlights of life force and consciousness are reversed. Withdrawing from the senses, they reveal the light of the spiritual eye.... Through this eye of omnipresence the devotee enters into the realms of divine consciousness.

❖ ❖ ❖

By the right method of meditation and devotion, with the eyes closed and concentrated on the spiritual eye, the devotee knocks at the gates of heaven. When the eyes are focused and still, and the breath and mind are calm, a light begins to form in the forehead. Eventually, with deep concentration, the tricolored light of the spiritual eye becomes visible.* Just seeing the single eye is not enough; it is more difficult for the devotee to go into that light. But by practice of the higher methods, such as *Kriya Yoga*, the consciousness is led inside the

---

* "The light of the body is the eye: if therefore thine eye be single, thy whole body shall be full of light" (Matthew 6:22).

spiritual eye, into another world of vaster dimensions.

In the gold halo of the spiritual eye, all creation is perceived as the vibratory light of the Holy Ghost. The blue light of Christ Consciousness is where the angels and deity agents of God's individualized powers of creation, preservation, and dissolution abide—as well as the most highly evolved saints. Through the white light of the spiritual eye, the devotee enters Cosmic Consciousness; he ascends unto God the Father.

❖ ❖ ❖

India's yogis (those who seek union with God through formal scientific methods of yoga) lay the utmost importance on keeping the spine straight during meditation, and upon concentrating on the point between the eyebrows. A bent spine during meditation offers real resistance to the process of reversing the life currents to flow upward towards the spiritual eye. A bent spine throws the vertebrae out of alignment and pinches the nerves, trapping the life force in its accustomed state of body consciousness and mental restlessness.

The populace in Israel was looking for Christ in a physical body, so John the Baptist assured them of the coming of one in whom Christ was manifested; but he also told them subtly that anyone who wanted truly to know Christ must receive him by uplifting the consciousness through the spine in meditation ("the way of the Lord").

John was emphasizing that just worshiping the body of Christ Jesus was not the way to know him. The Christ Consciousness embodied in Jesus could be realized only by awakening the astral centers of the spine, the straight way of ascension by which the metaphysical Christ Consciousness in the body of Jesus could be intuitionally perceived.

The words of the prophet Isaiah, which were echoed by John the Baptist, show that both knew that the subjective Lord of Finite Vibratory Creation, or Christ Consciousness, could be welcomed into one's own consciousness only through the meditation-awakened straight highway of the spine.

Isaiah, John, the yogis, all know that to receive Christ Consciousness more than a simple physical contact with a Christlike person is necessary. One must know how to meditate—how to switch off the attention from the distractions of the senses, and how to keep the consciousness fixed on the altar of the spiritual eye where Christ Consciousness can be received in all its glory.*

❖ ❖ ❖

Every true religion leads to God, but some paths take a longer time while others are shorter. No matter what God-ordained religion one follows, its beliefs will merge in one and the same common experience of God. Yoga is the unifying path that is followed by all religionists as they make the final approach to God. Before one can reach God, there has to be the "repentance" that turns the consciousness from delusive matter to the kingdom of God within. This withdrawal retires the life force and mind inward to rise through the spiritualizing centers of the spine to the supreme states of divine realization. The final union with God and the stages involved in this union are universal. That is yoga, the science of religion. Divergent bypaths will meet on the highway of God; and that highway is through the spine—the way to transcend body consciousness and enter the infinite divine kingdom.

❖ ❖ ❖

Spiritual truth and wisdom are found not in any words of a priest or preacher, but in the "wilderness" of inner silence. The Sanskrit scriptures say: "There are many sages with their scriptural and spiritual interpretations, apparently contradictory, but the real secret of religion is hidden in a cave." True religion lies within oneself, in the cave of stillness, in the cave of calm intuitive wisdom, in the cave of the spiritual eye. By concentrating on the point between the eyebrows and delving into the depths of quiet in the luminous spiritual eye, one can find answers to all the religious queries of the heart. "The Comforter, which is the Holy Ghost... shall teach you all things" (John 14:26).

---

* Whatever celestial star might have indicated to the Wise Men the birth of Jesus, it was a "star in the east" of greater power by which they knew of the coming on earth of Christ Jesus: the all-revealing light of the spiritual eye of the soul's intuitive divine perception located in the "east" of the body—in a subtle spiritual center of Christ Consciousness in the forehead between the two physical eyes.

Yoga Bestows the True Baptism in Spirit

The way of ascension was made manifest in the baptism of Jesus. As told in the Gospel According to Saint Matthew:

And Jesus, when he was baptized, went up straightway out of the water: and, lo, the heavens were opened unto him, and he saw the Spirit of God descending like a dove, and lighting upon him: And lo a voice from heaven, saying, "This is My beloved Son, in whom I am well pleased" (Matthew 3:16–17).

When one is baptized by immersion in the light of Spirit, the microcosmic spiritual eye in the body may be seen in its relation to the light of descending Spirit as the Cosmic Trinity. In the baptism of Jesus, this is described metaphorically as "Spirit descending like a dove, and lighting upon him." The dove symbolizes the spiritual eye, seen by deeply meditating devotees at the Christ Consciousness center in the forehead between the two physical eyes.

This eye of light and consciousness appears as a golden aura (the Holy Ghost Vibration) surrounding an opal-blue sphere (Christ Consciousness) in the center of which is a five-pointed star of brilliant white light (doorway to the Cosmic Consciousness of Spirit).

The threefold light of God in the spiritual eye is symbolized by a dove because it brings perennial peace. Also, looking in the spiritual eye produces in man's consciousness the purity signified by the dove.

The mouth of the symbolic dove represents the star in the spiritual eye, the secret passage to Cosmic Consciousness. The two wings of the dove represent the two spheres of consciousness emanating from Cosmic Consciousness: The blue light of the spiritual eye is the microcosm of the subjective Christ Intelligence in all creation; and the golden ring of light in the spiritual eye is the microcosmic objective cosmic energy, Cosmic Vibration, or Holy Ghost.

❖ ❖ ❖

During baptism by Spirit in the form of the Holy Ghost as experienced by Jesus, he saw the light of the spiritual eye as descended from the macrocosmic Divine Light; and from this came the voice of *Aum*, the intelligent, all-creative heavenly sound, vibrating as an intelligible voice:

"Thou art My Son, having lifted thy consciousness from the limitation of the body and all matter to realize thyself as one with My perfect reflection, My only begotten image, immanent in all manifestation. I am Bliss, and My joy I express in thy rejoicing in attunement with My Omnipresence."

Jesus felt his consciousness attuned to the Christ Consciousness, the "only begotten" reflection of God the Father's Intelligence in the Holy Vibration: he first felt his body as the entire vibratory creation in which his little body was included; then within his cosmic body of all creation, he experienced his oneness with God's innate Presence as the Infinite Christ or Universal Intelligence, a magnetic aura of blissful Divine Love in which God's presence holds all beings.

❖ ❖ ❖

In deepest meditation, as practiced by those who are advanced in the technique of *Kriya Yoga,* the devotee experiences not only expansion in the *Aum* vibration "Voice from heaven," but finds himself able also to follow the microcosmic light of Spirit in the "straight way" of the spine into the light of the spiritual eye "dove descending from heaven."...

Through his two physical eyes, man sees only his body and a little portion of the earth at a time. But spiritual baptism or initiation received from a true guru expands the consciousness. Anyone who can see, as did Jesus, the spiritual dove alight on him—that is, who can behold his spiritual eye of omnipresent omniscience—and through perseverance in ever deeper meditation penetrate his gaze through its light, will perceive the entire kingdom of Cosmic Energy and the consciousness of God existing within it and beyond, in the Infinite Bliss of Spirit.*

---

* In his *Autobiography of a Yogi,* Paramahansa Yogananda wrote: "The world illusion, *maya,* manifests in men as *avidya,* literally, 'not-knowledge,' ignorance, delusion. *Maya* or *avidya* can never be destroyed through intellectual conviction or analysis, but solely through attaining the interior state of *nirbikalpa samadhi.* The Old Testament prophets, and seers of all lands and ages, spoke from that state of consciousness.

"Ezekiel said: 'Afterwards he brought me to the gate, even the gate that looketh toward the east: and, behold, the glory of the God of Israel came from the way of the east: and his voice was like a noise of many waters: and the earth shined with his glory.' Through the divine eye in the forehead (east), the yogi sails his consciousness into omnipresence, hearing the Word or *Aum,* divine sound of 'many waters': the vibrations of light that constitute the sole reality of creation."

PART II

———◆━◗◆◖━◆———

"ONE WAY" OR UNIVERSALITY?

Jesus' Teachings on "Born Again,"
Attaining Heaven,
and "Belief on His Name"

———◆━◗◆◖━◆———

Christ at 33

"It is given unto you to know the mysteries of the kingdom of heaven...."

CHAPTER 4

The "Second Birth":
Awakening of Soul-Intuition

Hidden Truth in Jesus' Parables

And the disciples came, and said unto him, "Why speakest thou unto them in parables?" He answered and said unto them, "Because it is given unto you to know the mysteries of the kingdom of heaven, but to them it is not given....Therefore speak I to them in parables: because they seeing see not; and hearing they hear not, neither do they understand" (Matthew 13:10, 11, 13).

When Jesus was asked by his disciples why he taught the people in the subtle illustrations of parables, he answered, "Because it is so ordained that you who are my real disciples, living a spiritualized life and disciplining your actions according to my teachings, deserve by virtue of your inner awakening in your meditations to understand the truth of the arcane mysteries of heaven and how to attain the kingdom of God, Cosmic Consciousness hidden behind the vibratory creation of cosmic delusion.

"But ordinary people, unprepared in their receptivity, are not able either to comprehend or to practice the deeper wisdom-truths. From parables, they glean according to their understanding simpler truths from the wisdom I send out to them. By practical application of what they are able to receive, they make some progress toward redemption."...

How do the receptive perceive truth, whereas the unreceptive "seeing see not; and hearing they hear not, neither do they understand"? The ultimate truths of heaven and the kingdom of God, the reality that lies behind sensory perception and beyond the cogitations of the rationalizing

mind, can only be grasped by intuition—awakening the intuitive knowing, the pure comprehension, of the soul.

❖ ❖ ❖

*There was a man of the Pharisees, named Nicodemus, a ruler of the
Jews: The same came to Jesus by night, and said unto him, "Rabbi, we
know that thou art a teacher come from God: for no man can do these
miracles that thou doest, except God be with him."*

*Jesus answered and said unto him, "Verily, verily, I say unto thee,
except a man be born again, he cannot see the kingdom of God."*

*Nicodemus saith unto him, "How can a man be born when he is old?
Can he enter the second time into his mother's womb, and be born?"*

*Jesus answered, "Verily, verily, I say unto thee, except a man be born
of water and of the Spirit, he cannot enter into the kingdom of God.
That which is born of the flesh is flesh; and that which is born of the
Spirit is spirit. Marvel not that I said unto thee, 'Ye must be born again.'
The wind bloweth where it listeth, and thou hearest the sound thereof,
but canst not tell whence it cometh, and whither it goeth: so is every one
that is born of the Spirit" (John 3:1–8).*

Nicodemus visited Jesus secretly in the night, for he feared social
criticism. It was an act of courage for one of his position to approach
the controversial teacher and to declare his faith in Jesus' divine stature.
He reverently affirmed his conviction that only a master who had actual
God-communion could work the superlaws that govern the inner life of
all beings and all things.

In reply, Christ forthrightly directed Nicodemus' attention to the
heavenly Source of all phenomena in creation—mundane as well as
"miraculous"—pointing out succinctly that anyone can contact that
Source and know the wonders that proceed therefrom, even as Jesus
himself did, by undergoing the spiritual "second birth" of intuitional
soul-awakening.

The superficially curious crowds attracted by displays of phenomenal powers received only scantily from the wisdom trove of Jesus, but
the manifest sincerity of Nicodemus elicited from the Master determi-
nate guidance that emphasized the Supreme Power and Goal on which

man should concentrate. Miracles of wisdom to enlighten the mind are superior to miracles of physical healing and the subjugation of nature; and the even greater miracle is the healing of the root-cause of every form of suffering: delusive ignorance that obscures the unity of man's soul and God. That primordial forgetfulness is vanquished only by Self-realization, through the intuitive power by which the soul directly apprehends its own nature as individualized Spirit and perceives Spirit as the essence of everything.

All bona fide revealed religions of the world are based on intuitive knowledge. Each has an exoteric or outer particularity, and an esoteric or inner core. The exoteric aspect is the public image, and includes moral precepts and a body of doctrines, dogmas, dissertations, rules, and customs to guide the general populace of its followers. The esoteric aspect includes methods that focus on actual communion of the soul with God. The exoteric aspect is for the many; the esoteric is for the ardent few. It is the esoteric aspect of religion that leads to intuition, the firsthand knowledge of Reality.

The lofty *Sanatana Dharma* of the Vedic philosophy of ancient India—summarized in the Upanishads and in the six classical systems of metaphysical knowledge, and peerlessly encapsulated in the Bhagavad Gita—is based on intuitional perception of the Transcendental Reality. Buddhism, with its various methods of controlling the mind and gaining depth in meditation, advocates intuitive knowledge to realize the transcendence of *nirvana*. Sufism in Islam anchors on the intuitive mystical experience of the soul.* Within the Jewish religion are esoteric teachings based on inner experience of the Divine, evidenced abundantly in the legacy of the God-illumined Biblical prophets. Christ's teachings are fully expressive of that realization. The apostle John's Revelation is a remarkable disclosure of the soul's intuitional perception of deepest truths garbed in metaphor.

❖ ❖ ❖

* See Paramahansa Yogananda's *Wine of the Mystic: The Rubaiyat of Omar Khayyam—A Spiritual Interpretation* (published by Self-Realization Fellowship).

The "second birth," the necessity of which Jesus speaks, admits us to the land of intuitional perception of truth. The New Testament may not have been scribed with the word "intuition," but it is replete with references to intuitive knowledge. Indeed, the twenty-one verses describing Nicodemus' visit present, in condensed epigrammatic sayings so typical of Oriental scripture, Jesus' comprehensive esoteric teachings relating to the practical attainment of the infinite kingdom of blissful divine consciousness.

These verses have been largely interpreted in support of such doctrines as baptism of the body by water as a prerequisite for entering God's kingdom after death (John 3:5); that Jesus is the only "son of God" (John 3:16); that mere "belief" in Jesus is sufficient for salvation, and that all are condemned who do not so believe (John 3:17–18).

Such exoteric reading of scripture engulfs in dogma the universality of religion. A panorama of unity unfolds in an understanding of esoteric truth.

❖ ❖ ❖

"Except a man be born again, he cannot see the kingdom of God."

This choice of words by Jesus is an allusion to his familiarity with the Eastern spiritual doctrine of reincarnation. One meaning to be drawn from this precept is that the soul has to be born repeatedly in various bodies until it reawakens to realization of its native perfection. It is a false hope to believe that at bodily death the soul automatically enters into an everlasting angelic existence in heaven. Unless and until one attains perfection by removing the debris of karma (effects of one's actions) from the individualized God-image of his soul, he cannot enter God's kingdom.* The ordinary person, constantly creating new karmic bondage by his wrong actions and material desires, adding to the accumulated effects of numerous previous incarnations, cannot free his soul in one lifetime. It takes many lifetimes of physical, mental, and spiritual evolution to work out all karmic entanglements that block soul intuition, the pure knowing without which one cannot "see the kingdom of God."

---

* "Be ye therefore perfect, even as your Father in heaven is perfect" (Matthew 5:48).

The principal import of Jesus' words to Nicodemus goes beyond an implied reference to reincarnation. This is clear from Nicodemus' request for further explanation of how an *adult* could reach God's kingdom: Must he reenter his mother's womb and be reborn? Jesus elaborates in the succeeding verses as to how a person can be "born again" in his present incarnation—how a soul identified with the flesh and sense limitations can acquire by meditation a new birth in Cosmic Consciousness.

❖ ❖ ❖

"Except a man be born of water and of the Spirit, he cannot enter into the kingdom of God."

To be "born of water" is usually interpreted as a mandate for the outer ritual of baptism by water—a symbolic rebirth—in order to be eligible for God's kingdom after death. But Jesus did not mention a *re-birth* involving water. "Water" here means protoplasm; the body is made up mostly of water and begins its earthly existence in the amniotic fluid of the mother's womb. Though the soul has to go through the natural process of birth that God has established through His biological laws, physical birth is not enough for man to be fit to see or enter into the kingdom of God.

The ordinary consciousness is tied to the flesh, and through the two physical eyes man can see only into the diminutive playhouse of this earth and its encircling starry sky. Through the small outer windows of the five senses, body-bound souls perceive nothing of the wonders beyond limited matter.

When a person is high aloft in an airplane he sees no boundaries, only the limitlessness of space and free skies. But if he is caged in a room, surrounded by windowless walls, he loses the vision of vastness.

Similarly, when man's soul is sent out of the infinity of Spirit into a sensory-circumscribed mortal body, his outer experiences are confined to the limitations of matter. So Jesus alluded to the fact, as expressed by modern scientists, that we can see and know only as much as the limited instrumentality of the senses and reason allow.

Just as by a two-inch telescope the details of the distant stars cannot be seen, so Jesus was saying that man cannot see or know anything about the heavenly kingdom of God through the unaugmented power of his mind and senses. However, a 200-inch telescope enables man to peer into the vast reaches of star-peopled space; and similarly, by developing the intuitional sense through meditation he can behold and enter the causal and astral kingdom of God—birthplace of thoughts, stars, and souls.

Jesus points out that after man's soul becomes incarnate—born of water, or protoplasm—he should transcend the mortal impositions of the body by self-development. Through awakening the "sixth sense," intuition, and opening the spiritual eye, his illumined consciousness can enter into the kingdom of God. In this second birth the body remains the same; but the soul's consciousness, instead of being tied to the material plane, is free to roam in the boundless, eternally joyous empire of Spirit.

God intended His human children to live on earth with an awakened perception of the Spirit informing all creation, and thus to enjoy His dream-drama as a cosmic entertainment. Alone among living creatures, the human body was equipped, as a special creation of God, with the instruments and capacities necessary to express fully the soul's divine potentials. But through the delusion of Satan, man ignores his higher endowments and remains attached to the limited fleshly form and its mortality.

As individualized souls, Spirit progressively unfolds Its power of knowing through the successive stages of evolution: as unconscious response in minerals, as feeling in plant life, as instinctive sentient knowledge in animals, as intellect, reason, and undeveloped introspective intuition in man, and as pure intuition in the superman.

It is said that after eight million lives traveling the successive steps of upward evolution like a prodigal son through the cycles of incarnations, at last the soul arrives in a human birth. Originally, human beings were pure sons of God. Nobody knows the divine consciousness enjoyed by Adam and Eve except the saints. Ever since the Fall, man's misuse of his independence, he has lost that consciousness by associative equivalence of himself with the fleshly ego and its mortal desires. Not altogether uncommon are persons more like instinct-motivated animals than intellectually responsive human beings. They are so materially minded that when you talk about food or sex or money they understand and re-flexively respond, like Pavlov's famous salivating dog. But try to engage them in a meaningful philosophical exchange about God or the mystery of life, and their uncomprehending reaction is as though their conversationalist were crazy.

The spiritual man is trying to free himself from the materiality that is the cause of his prodigal wandering in the maze of incarnations, but the ordinary man does not want more than a betterment of his earthly existence. As instinct confines the animal within prescribed limits, so also does reason circumscribe the human being who does not try to be a superman by developing intuition. The person who worships reason only and is not conscious of the availability of his power of intuition—by which alone he can know himself as soul—remains little more than a rational animal, out of touch with the spiritual heritage that is his birthright.

❖ ❖ ❖

The body born of flesh has the limitations of the flesh, whereas the soul, born of the Spirit, has potentially limitless powers. By meditation, man's consciousness is transferred from the body to the soul, and through the soul's power of intuition he experiences himself not as a mortal body (a phenomenon of objective nature), but as immortal indwelling consciousness, one with the noumenal Divine Essence.

❖ ❖ ❖

Man remains firmly convinced that he is essentially a body, even though he daily receives proof to the contrary. Every night in sleep, "the little death," he discards his identification with the physical form and is reborn as invisible consciousness. Why is it that man is compelled to sleep? Because sleep is a reminder of what is beyond the state of sleep—the state of the soul. Mortal existence could not be borne without at least subconscious contact with the soul, which is provided by sleep.

At nighttime man dumps the body into the subconscious and becomes an angel; in the daytime he becomes once more a devil, divorced from Spirit by the desires and sensations of the body. By *Kriya Yoga* meditation he can be a god in the daytime, like Christ and the Great

Ones. He goes beyond the subconscious to the superconscious, and dissolves the consciousness of the body in the ecstasy of God. One who can do this is born again.

❖ ❖ ❖

This earth is a habitat of trouble and suffering, but the kingdom of God that is behind this material plane is an abode of freedom and bliss. The soul of the awakening man has followed a hard-earned way—many incarnations of upward evolution—in order to arrive at the human state and the possibility to reclaim his lost divinity. Yet how many human births have been wasted in preoccupation with food and money and gratification of the body and egoistic emotions! Each person should ask himself how he is using the precious moments of this present birth. Eventually the bodies of all human beings fall painfully apart; isn't it better to separate the soul from the body consciousness—to keep the body as the temple of the Spirit? O Soul, you are not the body; why not remember always that you are the Spirit of God?*

Jesus said that we must reestablish our connection with Eternity; we must be born again. Man has either to follow the circuitous route of reincarnations to work out his karma, or—by a technique such as *Kriya Yoga* and the help of a true guru—to awaken the divine faculty of intuition and know himself as a soul, that is, be born again in Spirit. By the latter method he can see and enter the kingdom of God in this lifetime.

Sooner or later, after a few or many painful incarnations, the soul in every human being will cry out to remind him that his home is not here, and he will begin in earnest to retrace his steps to his rightful heavenly kingdom. When one is very desirous to know Truth, God sends a master through whose devotion and realization He plants His love in that person's heart.

Human birth is given by one's parents; but the spiritual birth is given by the God-ordained guru. In the Vedic tradition of ancient India, the newly born child is called *kayastha*, which means "body identified." The two physical eyes, which look into alluring matter, are bequeathed by the

---

* "Know ye not that ye are the temple of God, and that the Spirit of God dwelleth in you?" (I Corinthians 3:16).

physical parents; but at the time of initiation, spiritual baptism, the spiritual eye is opened by the guru. Through the help of the guru, the initiate learns to use this telescopic eye to see Spirit, and then becomes *dwija,* "twice-born"—the same metaphysical terminology used by Jesus—and begins his progress toward the state of becoming a *Brahmin,* one who knows Brahman or Spirit.

The matter-bound soul, lifted into the Spirit by God-contact, is born a second time, in Spirit. Alas, even in India this initiation from body consciousness to spiritual consciousness has become just a formality, a caste ceremony performed on young Brahmin boys by ordinary priests—tantamount to the symbolic ritual of baptism with water. But Jesus, like great Hindu masters of ancient and modern times, conferred the actual baptism of Spirit—"with the Holy Ghost, and with fire." A true guru is one who can change the disciple's brain cells by the spiritual current flowing from God through his enlightened consciousness. All will feel that change who are in tune—who meditate sincerely and deeply and, as in the practice of *Kriya Yoga,* learn to send the divine current into the brain cells. The soul is bound to the body by cords of karma, woven by lifetimes of material desires, behavior, and habits. Only the life current can change one's life, destroying those millions of karmic records. Then one is born again; the soul opens the inner window of oneness with the Spirit and enters into the perception of the wondrous omnipresence of God.

So the term "born again" means much more than merely joining a church and receiving ceremonial baptism. Belief alone will not give the soul a permanent place in heaven after death; it is necessary to have communion with God now. Human beings are made angels on earth, not in heaven. At death, wherever one leaves off in his progress, he will have to start in again in a new incarnation. After sleep one is the same as before sleep; after death one is the same as before death.

That is why Christ and the Masters say it is necessary to become saintly before the sleep of death. It cannot be done by filling the mind with mortal attachments and useless diversions. One who is engrossed in storing up treasure on earth is not busy with God; one who is intent on God does not want many fillers in his life. It is by freeing oneself from earthly desires that one gains entry into the kingdom of God. The Lord patiently waits for one hundred percent of man's devotion; for those who diligently seek Him every day, and who fulfill His commandments through godly behavior, He opens the door to the kingdom of His presence.

A multitude of lectures about sunshine and scenic beauties will not enable me to see them if my eyes are closed. So it is that people do not see God who is omnipresent in everything unless and until they open their spiritual eye of intuitive perception. When one can perceive that he is not the mortal body but a spark of the Infinite Spirit cloaked in a concentration of life energy, then he will be able to see the kingdom of God. He will realize that the composition of his body and the universe is not soul-imprisoning matter, but expansive, indestructible energy and consciousness. Science has proved this truth; and each individual can experience it. Through *Kriya Yoga*, he can have the unshakable realization that he is that great Light and Consciousness of Spirit.

O man, how long will you remain a rational animal? How long will you fruitlessly try to look into the endless tracts of creation with only your myopic eyes of senses and reason? How long will you remain bound to satisfying the demands of animal man? Shed all constraining fetters; know yourself as something immortal, having limitless powers and faculties. No more this age-old dream of rational animal! Wake up! you are the intuitional child of immortality!

CHAPTER 5

"Lifting Up the Son of Man" to Divine Consciousness

Nicodemus answered and said unto him, "How can these things be?"

Jesus answered and said unto him, "Art thou a master of Israel, and knowest not these things? Verily, verily, I say unto thee, we speak that we do know, and testify that we have seen; and ye receive not our witness. If I have told you earthly things, and ye believe not, how shall ye believe, if I tell you of heavenly things?

"And no man hath ascended up to heaven, but he that came down from heaven, even the Son of man which is in heaven. And as Moses lifted up the serpent in the wilderness, even so must the Son of man be lifted up: that whosoever believeth in him should not perish, but have eternal life" (John 3:9–15).

Jesus, in addressing Nicodemus, observed that merely holding the ceremonial office of a master of the house of Israel did not guarantee an understanding of the mysteries of life. Often persons are accorded religious titles by virtue of intellectual knowledge of the scriptures; but a full comprehension of the esoteric depths of truth can be known only by intuitive experience.

"We speak that we do know" is knowledge deeper than the information derived through sensory-dependent intellect and reason. Since the senses are limited, so is intellectual understanding. The senses and mind are the outer doors through which knowledge percolates into the consciousness. Human knowledge filters in through the senses and is interpreted by the mind. If the senses err in perception, the conclusion drawn by the understanding of that data is also incorrect.

A white gossamer cloth fluttering in the distance may look like a ghost, and a superstitious person believes that it is a ghost; but closer observation reveals the error of that conclusion. The senses and understanding are easily deluded because they cannot grasp the real nature, the essential character and substance, of created things.

Jesus, with his intuition, had full realization of the noumena supporting the workings of the cosmos and its diversity of life, so he said authoritatively: *"We do know."*

Jesus was attuned to the grand scheme of manifestation behind all space, behind earthly vision. To belligerent minds he could not speak openly of his omnipresent perceptions—even the truths he did tell brought crucifixion! He said to Nicodemus: "If I tell you about matters pertaining to human souls who are visibly present on earth, and how they can enter into the kingdom of God, and you believe not, then how can you believe me if I tell you about happenings in the heavenly realms, which are completely hidden from the ordinary human gaze?"

Though Jesus regretted, with accommodating patience, that Nicodemus doubted the intuitional revelations of the Christ state, he went on to tell his visitor the way in which he—and any other seeker of truth—could experience these truths for himself.

So many doubt heaven because they do not see it. Yet they do not doubt the breeze simply because it is unseen. It is known by its sound and sensation on the skin and the motion in the leaves and other objects. The whole universe lives, moves, breathes because of the invisible presence of God in the heavenly forces behind matter.

Once a man gave some olives to another who had never seen olives, and said, "These have a lot of oil in them." The person cut the fruit but could see no oil—until his friend showed him how to squeeze the olives in order to extract the oil from the pulp. So it is with God. Everything in the universe is saturated with His presence—the twinkling stars, the rose, the song of the bird, our minds. His Being permeates everything, everywhere. But one has metaphorically to "squeeze" God out of His material concealment.

Inner concentration is the way to realize the subtle, prolific heaven behind this gross universe. Seclusion is the price of greatness and God-contact.

All who are willing to snatch time from the greedy material world to devote it instead to the divine search can learn to behold the wondrous factory of creation out of which all things are born. From the heavenly causal and astral spheres every physically incarnate soul has descended, and every soul can reascend by retreating to the "wilderness" of interior silence and practicing the scientific method of lifting up the life force and consciousness from body identification to union with God.

❖ ❖ ❖

"And no man hath ascended up to heaven, but he that came down from heaven, even the Son of man which is in heaven. And as Moses lifted up the serpent in the wilderness, even so must the Son of man be lifted up" (John 3:13–14).

This passage is very important, and little understood. Taken literally, the words "lifted up the serpent" are at best a classic scriptural ambiguity. Every symbol has a hidden meaning that must be rightly interpreted.

The word "serpent" here refers metaphorically to man's consciousness and life force in the subtle coiled passageway at the base of the spine, the matterward flow of which is to be reversed for man to reascend from body attachment to superconscious freedom.

As souls we were all originally in God's bosom. Spirit projects the desire to create an individualized expression of Itself. The soul becomes manifest and projects the idea of the body in causal form. The idea becomes energy, or the lifetronic astral body. The astral body becomes condensed into the physical body. Through the integrated spinal passageway of these three instrumental media, the soul descends into identification with the material body and gross matter.

"He that came down from heaven" means the physical body. (Jesus refers to the human body as "man"; throughout the Gospels he spoke of his own physical body as "the Son of man," as distinguished from his Christ Consciousness, "the Son of God.") Man descends from the heavenly planes of God's creation when his soul, garbed in its causal body of God-congealed ideas and its astral body of light, takes on an outer covering of material tissue. So not only Jesus but all of God's children have "come down from heaven."

❖ ❖ ❖

No human body has ascended into heaven, the etheric essence of which does not accommodate corporeal forms; but all souls can and will enter the supernal realms when, through death or through spiritual transcendence, they cast off physical consciousness and know themselves as angelic beings garbed in thought and light.

We are all made in the image of God, beings of immortal consciousness cloaked in diaphanous heavenly light—a heritage buried beneath the cloddish flesh. That heritage we can only acknowledge by meditation. There is no other way—not by reading books, not by philosophical study, but by devotion and continuous prayer and scientific meditation that uplifts the consciousness to God.

❖ ❖ ❖

Jesus spoke of an extraordinary truth when he mentioned "the Son of man which is in heaven." Ordinary souls behold their bodies ("Son of man") roaming only on the earth, but free souls such as Jesus dwell simultaneously in the physical and in the astral and causal heavenly kingdoms....

So Jesus' words are very simple and very wonderful: Even while dwelling in a body in the physical world, he was beholding himself as a ray of God descending from heaven. He demonstrated this conclusively after his death, re-creating his physical body from rays of cosmic creative light, and later dematerializing it in the presence of his disciples when he ascended back to heaven....

While Jesus, in his God-ordained incarnation, was effectually engaged in his Heavenly Father's work in the world, he could in truth proclaim: "I am in heaven." This is the highest ecstasy of God-consciousness, defined by yogis as *nirvikalpa samadhi,* an ecstatic state "without difference" between external consciousness and interior God-union. In *savikalpa samadhi,* "with difference," a less exalted state, one is not conscious of the outer world; the body enters an inert trance while the awareness is immersed in interior conscious oneness with God. The most advanced masters can be fully conscious of God and not show any signs of the body being transfixed; the devotee drinks God and simultaneously is conscious and fully active in his external environment—if he so chooses.

This declaration of Jesus offers great encouragement to every soul: Although man is beset with the perplexities that accompany residence in a physical body, God has provided him with the potential to remain in heavenly consciousness regardless of outer circumstances. An inebriate takes his drunkenness with him no matter where he goes. One who is sick is all the time preoccupied with his sickness. One who is happy is ever bubbling with good cheer. And the one who is conscious of God enjoys that supreme Bliss whether he is active in the outer world or absorbed in inner communion.

❖ ❖ ❖

Again and again in the Gospels, Jesus emphasizes that what he attained, all may attain. His next remark to Nicodemus shows how.

"And as Moses lifted up the serpent in the wilderness, even so must the Son of man be lifted up: that whosoever believeth in him should not perish, but have eternal life."

Jesus said that each son of man, each bodily consciousness, must be lifted from the plane of the senses to the astral kingdom by reversing the matter-bent outflowing of the life force to ascension through the serpent-like coiled passage at the base of the spine—the son of man is lifted up when this serpentine force is uplifted, "as Moses lifted up the serpent in the wilderness." We must reascend, just as Moses, in the spiritual wilderness of silence in which all his desires were no more, lifted his soul from body consciousness into God-consciousness through the same path by which it had descended.

As explained earlier, man's physical, astral, and causal bodies are tied together and work as one by a knotting of life force and consciousness in the seven cerebrospinal centers. In descending order, the final tie is a coiled knot at the base of the spine, preventing the ascension of consciousness into the heavenly astral kingdom. Unless one knows how to open this knot of astral and physical power, the life and consciousness remain attracted to the mortal realm, emanating outward into the body and sensory consciousness.

Most energy moves through space in a spiral form—a ubiquitous motif in the macrocosmic and microscopic architecture of the universe.

Beginning with galactic nebulae—the cosmic birth-cradle of all matter—energy flows in coiled or circular or vortex-like patterns. The theme
is repeated in the orbital dance of electrons around their atomic nucleus,
and (as cited in Hindu scriptures of ancient origin) of planets and suns
and stellar systems spinning through space around a grand center of
the universe. Many galaxies are spiral-shaped; and countless other phenomena in nature—plants, animals, the winds and storms—similarly
evidence the invisible whorls of energy underlying their shape and structure. Such is the "serpent force" (*kundalini*) in the microcosm of the
human body: the coiled current at the base of the spine, a tremendous
dynamo of life that when directed outward sustains the physical body
and its sensory consciousness; and when consciously directed upward,
opens the wonders of the astral cerebrospinal centers.

When the soul, in its subtle sheaths of causal and astral bodies, enters physical incarnation at the time of conception, the entire body grows
from the seed cell formed from the united sperm and ovum, beginning
with the first vestiges of the medulla oblongata, brain, and spinal cord.

From its original seat in the medulla, the intelligent life energy of
the astral body flows downward—activating the specialized powers in
the astral cerebrospinal *chakras* that create and give life to the physical
spine, nervous system, and all other bodily organs. When the work of
the primal life force in creating the body is complete, it comes to rest in
a coiled passage in the lowest, or coccygeal, center. The coiled configuration in this astral center gives to the life energy therein the terminology of
kundalini or serpent force (from Sanskrit *kundala,* "coiled"). Its creative
work completed, the concentration of life force in this center is said to
be "sleeping" *kundalini,* for as it emanates outward into the body, continuously enlivening the physical region of the senses—of sight, hearing,
smell, taste, and touch, and of the earthbound physical creative force of
sex—it causes the consciousness to become strongly identified with the
delusive dreams of the senses and their domain of activity and desires.

Moses, Jesus, the Hindu yogis, all knew the secret of scientific spiritual life. They unanimously demonstrated that every person who is yet
physically minded must master the art of lifting up the serpent force

from sensory body consciousness in order to accomplish the first retracing of the inward steps toward Spirit.

Any saint of any religion who has attained God-consciousness has, in effect, withdrawn his consciousness and life force from the sense regions up through the spinal passage and plexuses to the center of God-consciousness in the brain, and thence into omnipresent Spirit.

When one is sitting quietly and calmly, he has partially stilled the life force flowing out into the nerves, releasing it from the muscles; for the moment his body is relaxed. But his peace is easily disturbed by any noise or other sensation that reaches him, because the life energy that continues to flow outward through the coiled path keeps the senses operative.

In sleep, the astral life forces are withdrawn not only from the muscles but also from the sensory instruments. Every night each man accomplishes a physical withdrawal of the life force, albeit in an unconscious way; the energy and consciousness in the body retire to the region of the heart, spine, and brain, giving man the rejuvenating peace of subconscious contact with the divine dynamo of all his powers, the soul. Why does man feel joy in sleep? Because when he is in the stage of deep, dreamless sleep, unconscious of the body, physical limitations are forgotten and the mind momentarily taps a higher consciousness.

The yogi knows the scientific art of withdrawing consciously from his sensory nerves, so that no outer disturbance of sight, sound, touch, taste, or smell can gain entry into the inner sanctum of his peace-saturated meditation. Soldiers posted for days on the front lines are able to fall asleep despite the constant roar of battle, because of the body's mechanism of unconsciously withdrawing the energy from the ears and other sensory organs. The yogi reasons that this can be done consciously. By knowledge and practice of the definite laws and scientific techniques of concentration, yogis switch off the senses at will—going beyond subconscious slumber into blissful superconscious interiorization.

❖ ❖ ❖

Every human being has learned to enter subconsciousness in sleep; and everyone can likewise master the art of superconscious ecstasy, with its infinitely more enjoyable and restorative experience than can be gleaned from sleep. That higher state bestows the constant aware-ness that matter is the frozen imaginings of God, as in sleep our dreams and nightmares are our own ephemeral thought-creations, condensed or "frozen" into visual experiences through the objectifying power of our imagination. A dreaming person does not know that a nightmare is unreal until he wakes up. So also, only by awakening in Spirit—oneness with God in *samadhi*—can man disperse the cosmic dream from the screen of his individualized consciousness.

Ascension in Spirit is not easy, because when one is conscious of the body he is in the grip of his second nature of insistent moods and habits. Without timidity, one must vanquish the desires of the body. A body-bound "son of man" cannot ascend to heavenly freedom just by talking about it; he has to know how to open the coiled knot of *kundalini* force at the base of the spine in order to transcend the confinement of the fleshly prison.

Every time one meditates deeply, he automatically helps to reverse the life force and consciousness from matter to God. If the current in the astral knot at the base of the spine is not lifted up by good living, good thoughts, meditation, then materialistic thoughts, worldly thoughts, base thoughts, are emphasized in one's life. With every good act man performs he is "ascending to heaven"—his mind becoming more fo-cused at the Christ Center of heavenly perception; with every evil act he is descending into matter, his attention captivated by the phantoms of delusion.

❖ ❖ ❖

Awakening the *kundalini* force is exceedingly difficult and cannot be done accidentally. It takes years of concerted meditation under the guid-ance of a competent guru before one can dream of releasing the heavenly astral body from its bondage to physical confinement by awakening the *kundalini*. One who is able to awaken the *kundalini* fast approaches the state of Christhood. Ascension through that coiled pathway opens the spiritual eye of spherical vision, revealing the whole universe surround-ing the body, supported by the vibratory light of heavenly powers.

The senses of sight, hearing, taste, touch, and smell are like five searchlights revealing matter. As the life energy pours outward through those sensory beams, man is attracted by beautiful faces or captivating sounds or enticing scents, flavors, and tactual sensations. It is natural; but what is natural to the body-bound consciousness is unnatural to the soul. But when that divine life energy is withdrawn from the autocratic senses, through the spinal path into the spiritual center of infinite perception in the brain, then the searchlight of astral energy is cast onto the boundlessness of eternity to reveal the universal Spirit. The devotee is then attracted by the Supernal Supernatural, the Beauty of all beauties, the Music of all music, the Joy of all joys. He can touch Spirit all over the universe and can hear the voice of God reverberating throughout the spheres. The form dissolves in the Formless. The consciousness of the body, confined to a temporal, little form, illimitably expands into the formless, ever-existing Spirit.

Jesus explains that whosoever believes in the doctrine of lifting the bodily consciousness (son of man) from the physical to the astral by reversing the life force through the coiled passage at the base of the spine, will not perish, that is, be subject to mortal changes of life and death, but will gradually acquire the immutable state—Christ Consciousness, the Son of God.

CHAPTER 6

The True Meaning of
"Belief on His Name" and Salvation

"For God so loved the world, that He gave his only begotten Son, that whosoever believeth in him should not perish, but have everlasting life. For God sent not His Son into the world to condemn the world; but that the world through him might be saved. He that believeth on him is not condemned: but he that believeth not is condemned already, because he hath not believed in the name of the only begotten Son of God.

"And this is the condemnation, that light is come into the world, and men loved darkness rather than light, because their deeds were evil. For every one that doeth evil hateth the light, neither cometh to the light, lest his deeds should be reproved. But he that doeth truth cometh to the light, that his deeds may be made manifest, that they are wrought in God" (John 3:16–21).

The confusion between "Son of man" and "only begotten Son of God" has created much bigotry in the community of churchianity, which does not understand or acknowledge the human element in Jesus—that he was a man, born in a mortal body, who had evolved his consciousness to become one with God Himself. Not the body of Jesus but the consciousness within it was one with the only begotten Son, the Christ Consciousness, the only reflection of God the Father in creation. In urging people to believe in the only begotten Son, Jesus was referring to this Christ Consciousness, which was fully manifest within himself and all God-realized masters throughout the ages, and is latent within every soul. Jesus said that all souls who lift their physical consciousness (Son of man consciousness) to the astral heaven, and then become one with the only begotten Christ Intelligence in all creation, will know eternal life.

Does this Bible passage mean that all who do not accept or believe in Jesus as their Savior will be condemned? This is a dogmatic concept of condemnation. What Jesus meant was that whoever does not realize himself as one with the universal Christ Consciousness is condemned to live and think as a struggling mortal, delimited by sensory boundaries, because he has essentially disunited himself from the Eternal Principle of life.

Jesus never referred to his Son-of-man consciousness, or to his body, as the only savior throughout all time. Abraham and many others were saved even before Jesus was born. It is a metaphysical error to speak of the historical person of Jesus as the only savior. It is the Christ Intelligence that is the universal redeemer. As the sole reflection of the Absolute Spirit (the Father) ubiquitous in the world of relativity, the Infinite Christ is the one mediator or link between God and matter, through which all matter-formed individuals—irrespective of different castes and creeds—must pass in order to reach God. All souls can free their matter-confined consciousness and plunge it into the vastness of Omnipresence by tuning in with Christ Consciousness.

Jesus said: "When ye have lifted up the Son of man, then shall ye know that I am he." He realized that his physical body was to remain on the earth plane for only a little while, so he made clear to those for whom he was the savior that when his body (son of man) was gone from the earth, people would still be able to find God and salvation by believing in and knowing the omnipresent only begotten Son of God. Jesus emphasized that whosoever would believe in his spirit as the Infinite Christ incarnate in him would discover the path to eternal life through the meditative science of interiorized ascension of the consciousness.

"That whosoever believeth in him should not perish." The forms of nature change, but the Infinite Intelligence immanent in nature is ever unchanged by the mutations of delusion. A child who is temperamentally attached to a snowman will cry when the sun rises high in the heavens and melts that form. Likewise do the children of God suffer who are attached to the mutable human body, which passes through infancy, youth, old age, and death. But those who interiorize their life force and consciousness and concentrate on the inner soul-spark of immortality

perceive heaven even while on earth; and, realizing the transcendent essence of life, they are not subject to the pain and suffering inherent in the incessant cycles of life and death.*

Jesus' majestic words in this passage were meant to convey a divinely encouraging promise of redemption to all humanity. Instead, centuries of misinterpretion have instigated wars of intolerant hatred, torturous inquisitions, and divisive condemnations.

"For God sent not His Son into the world to condemn the world; but that the world through him might be saved." "The world" in this verse means the whole of God's creation. The Lord's purpose in reflecting His Intelligence in creation, making a structured cosmos possible, was not to devise a jailhouse of finitude where souls are confined as willy-nilly participants in the *danse macabre* of suffering and destruction, but to make Himself accessible as an impelling Force to urge the world from ignorance-darkened material manifestation to an illumined spiritual manifestation.

It is true that the vibratory creative manifestation of the Universal Intelligence has originated the myriad attractions of the cosmic playhouse through which man is constantly bemused to move away from the Spirit to material life, to turn away from the Universal Love to the infatuations of human life. Still, perception of the Absolute beyond creation is intimately close through the intermediary of Its reflected Intelligence in creation. Through this contact, the devotee realizes that God sent the Christ Intelligence (His only begotten Son) to produce not a torture chamber but a colossal cosmic motion picture, whose scenes and actors would entertain for a time and ultimately return to the Bliss of Spirit.

In the light of that understanding, regardless of one's circumstances in this relative world, one feels his connection with the Universal Spirit and apprehends the vast Intelligence of the Absolute working in all

---

* "The heavens shall be rolled back, and the earth unfurled before your eyes. The one who has life from the Living One sees neither death nor fear." —Gospel According to Thomas, verse 111 (*Publisher's Note*)

　　Lord Krishna in the Bhagavad Gita (II: 40) speaks thus about the yoga science: "Even a tiny bit of this real religion protects one from great fear (the colossal sufferings inherent in the repeated cycles of birth and death)."

Dogma and Politics: How the True Meaning of "Only Begotten Son" Was Lost

As with "the Word" (see Chapter 3), the "only begotten Son" only came to signify the person of Jesus through a gradual evolution of doctrine brought about by complex theological and political influences. For a detailed history, see, for example, *When Jesus Became God: The Struggle to Define Christianity During the Last Days of Rome* by Richard E. Rubenstein (New York: Harcourt, 1999).

The writings of many gnostic Christians from the first two centuries A.D., including Basilides, Theodotus, Valentinus, and Ptolemaeus, similarily express an understanding of the "only begotten Son" as a cosmic principle in creation—the divine *Nous* (Greek for intelligence, mind, or thought)—rather than as the person of Jesus.

The celebrated church father Clement of Alexandria quotes from the writings of Theodotus that "the only begotten Son is *Nous*" (*Excerpta ex Theodoto* 6.3). In *Gnosis: A Selection of Gnostic Texts* (Oxford, England: Clarendon Press, 1972), German scholar Werner Foerster quotes Irenaeus as saying: "Basilides presents *Nous* originating first from the unoriginate Father." Valentinus, a teacher greatly respected by the Christian congregation in Rome around A.D. 140, held similar views, according to Foerster, believing that "in the Prologue to the Gospel of John, the 'Only-begotten' takes the place of *Nous*."

At the Council of Nicaea (A.D. 325), however, and at the later Council of Constantinople (A.D. 381) the church proclaimed as official doctrine that Jesus himself was, in the words of the Nicene Creed, "the only begotten Son of God, begotten from the Father before all ages, light from light, true God from true God, begotten not made, *homoousios* ['of one substance'] with the Father." After the Council of Constantinople, writes Timothy D. Barnes in *Athanasius and Constantius: Theology and Politics in the Constantinian Empire* (Harvard University Press, 1993), "the emperor enshrined its decisions in law, and he subjected Christians who did not accept the creed of Nicaea and its watchword *homoousios* to legal disabilities. As has long been recognized, these events marked the transition from one distinctive epoch in the history of the Christian church and the Roman Empire to another."

From that point on, explains Richard E. Rubenstein in *When Jesus Became God,* the official teaching of the church was that to not accept Jesus as God was to reject God Himself. Through the centuries, this view had enormous and often tragic implications for the relationship between Christians and Jews (and later, Muslims, who regarded Jesus as a divine prophet but not as part of the Godhead), as well as for the non-Christian peoples in the lands later conquered and colonized by European nations. *(Publisher's Note)*

the relativities of Nature. Anyone who believes in and concentrates on that Intelligence—Christ—instead of Its products—the external creation—finds redemption.

To think that the Lord condemns nonbelievers as sinners is incongruous. Since the Lord Himself dwells in all beings, condemnation would be utterly self-defeating. God never punishes man for not believing in Him; man punishes himself. If one does not believe in the dynamo and cuts the wires that connect his home to that source, he forfeits the advantages of that electrical power. Likewise, to disavow the Intelligence that is omnipresent in all creation is to deny the consciousness its link with the Source of divine wisdom and love that empowers the process of ascension in Spirit.

Recognition of the immanence of God can begin as simply as expanding one's love in an ever-widening circle. Man condemns himself to limitation whenever he thinks solely of his own little self, his own family, his own nation. Inherent in the evolution of nature and man back to God is the process of expansion. The exclusivity of family consciousness—"us four and no more"—is wrong. To shut out the larger family of humanity is to shut out the Infinite Christ. One who disconnects himself from the happiness and welfare of others has already condemned himself by isolation from the Spirit that pervades all souls, for he who does not extend himself in love and service to God in others disregards the redeeming power of connection with the universality of Christ. Each human being has been given the power to do good; if he fails to utilize that attribute, his level of spiritual evolution is little better than the instinctive self-interest of the animal.

Pure love in human hearts radiates the universal Christ-love. To expand continuously the circle of one's love is to attune human consciousness with the only begotten Son. Loving family members is the first step in expanding self-love to those nearby; loving all human beings of whatever race and nationality is to know Christ-love.

It is God alone as the Omnipresent Christ who is responsible for all expressions of life. The Lord is painting glorious scenery in the ever-changing clouds and sky. He is creating altars of His fragrant loveliness in the flowers. In everything and everyone—friends and enemies;

mountains, forests, ocean, air, the wheeling galactic canopy overarching all—the Christ-devotee sees the one blended light of God. He finds that the myriad expressions of the one Light, often seemingly chaotic in conflict and contradictions, were created by God's intelligence not to delude human beings or to afflict them, but to coax them to seek the Infinite whence they have emerged. One who looks not to the parts but to the whole discerns the purpose of creation: that without exception we are moving inexorably toward universal salvation. All rivers are moving toward the ocean; the rivers of our lives are moving toward God.

The waves on the surface of the ocean constantly change as they sport with the wind and tidal elements, but their oceanic essence remains constant. He who concentrates on one isolated wave of life will suffer, because that wave is unstable and will not last. This is what Jesus meant by "condemned": Body-bound man creates his own condemnation by isolating himself from God. To be saved he must reestablish his realization of inseparable unity with the Divine Immanence.

"In waking, eating, working, dreaming, sleeping,
Serving, meditating, chanting, divinely loving,
My soul constantly hums, unheard by any:
God! God! God!"*

In this way one remains continually aware of his connection with the changeless Divine Intelligence—the Absolute Goodness underlying the provocative riddles of creation.

"He that believeth on him is not condemned; but he that believeth not is condemned already." This highlights also the role of "belief" in the condemnation or noncondemnation of man. Persons who do not understand the immanence of the Absolute in the relative world tend to become either skeptical or dogmatic, because in both cases religion is a matter of blind beliefs. Unable to reconcile the idea of a good God with the seeming evils in creation, the skeptic rejects religious belief as stubbornly as the dogmatist clings to it.

The truths taught by Jesus went far beyond blind belief, which waxes and wanes under the influence of the paradoxical pronouncements of

---

* From *Songs of the Soul* by Paramahansa Yogananda (published by Self-Realization Fellowship).

priest and cynic. Belief is an initial stage of spiritual progress necessary to receive the concept of God. But that concept has to be transposed into conviction, into experience. Belief is the precursor of conviction; one has to believe a thing in order to investigate equitably about it. But if one is satisfied only with belief, it becomes dogma—narrow-mindedness, a preclusion of truth and spiritual progress. What is necessary is to grow, in the soil of belief, the harvest of direct experience and contact of God. That indisputable realization, not mere belief, is what saves people.

If someone says to me, "I believe in God," I will ask him, "Why do you believe? How do you know there is a God?" If the reply is based on supposition or secondhand knowledge, I will say that he does not truly believe. To hold a conviction one must have some data to support it; otherwise it is mere dogma, and is easy prey for skepticism.

If I were to point to a piano and proclaim that it is an elephant, the reason of an intelligent person would revolt against this absurdity. Likewise when dogmas about God are propagated without the validation of experience or realization, sooner or later when tested with a contrary experience reason will assail with speculation the truth about those ideas. As the scorching rays of the sun of analytical inquiry get hotter and hotter, frail unsubstantiated beliefs wilt and wither away, leaving a wasteland of doubt, agnosticism, or atheism.

Transcending mere philosophy, scientific meditation attunes the consciousness to the highest mighty truth; with every step the devotee moves toward actual realization and avoids bewildered wandering. To persevere in efforts to verify and experience beliefs through intuitional realization, which can be attained by yoga methods, is to build a real spiritual life that is proof against doubt.

Belief is a powerful force if it leads to the desire and determination to experience Christ. This is what Jesus meant when he urged people to "believe in the name of the only begotten Son of God": Through meditation, withdraw the consciousness and life energy from the senses and matter to intuit the *Aum*, the Word or all-pervading Cosmic Vibratory Energy that is the "name" or active manifestation of the immanent Christ Consciousness. One can assert incessantly an intellectual belief in Jesus Christ; but if he never actually experiences the Cosmic Christ, as both omnipresent and incarnate in Jesus, the spiritual practicality of his belief is insufficient to save him.

No one can be saved just by repeatedly uttering the Lord's name or praising Him in crescendos of hallelujahs. Not in blind belief in the name of Jesus or the adoration of his personality can the liberating power of his teachings be received. The real worship of Christ is the divine communion of Christ-perception in the wall-less temple of expanded consciousness.

God would not reflect His "only begotten Son" in the world to act like an implacable detective to track down unbelievers for punishment. The redeeming Christ Intelligence, abiding in the bosom of every soul regardless of its bodily accumulation of sins or virtues, waits with infinite patience for each one to awaken in meditation from delusion-drugged sleep to receive the grace of salvation. The person who believes in this Christ Intelligence, and who cultivates with spiritual action the desire to seek salvation through ascension in this reflected consciousness of God, no longer has to wander blindly along the delusive path of error. By measured steps he moves surely toward the redeeming Infinite Grace. But the unbeliever who scorns the thought of this Savior, the only way of salvation, condemns himself to body-bound ignorance and its consequences, until he awakens spiritually.

❖ ❖ ❖

"And this is the condemnation, that light is come into the world, and men loved darkness rather than light, because their deeds were evil. For every one that doeth evil hateth the light, neither cometh to the light, lest his deeds should be reproved. But he that doeth truth cometh to the light, that his deeds may be made manifest, that they are wrought in God" (John 3:19–21).

The all-pervading light of God, imbued with the universal Christ Intelligence, silently emanates divine love and wisdom to guide all beings back to the Infinite Consciousness. The soul, being a microcosm of Spirit, is an ever present light in man to lead him through discriminative intelligence and the intuitive voice of conscience; but all too often the rationalization of desireful habits and whims refuses to follow. Tempted by the Satan of cosmic delusion, man chooses actions that obliterate the light of discriminative inner guidance.

The origin of sin and its resultant physical, mental, and spiritual suffering therefore lies in the fact that the soul's divine intelligence and discrimination are suppressed by man's misuse of his God-given free choice. Though nonunderstanding people ascribe to God their own vengeful propensities, the "condemnation" of which Jesus spoke is not punishment meted out by a tyrannical Creator, but the results man brings on himself by his own actions, according to the law of cause and effect (karma) and the law of habit.

Succumbing to desires that keep their consciousness concentrated on and confined in the material world—the "darkness" or gross portion of cosmic creation in which the illumining Divine Presence is heavily obscured by the shadows of *maya*-delusion—benighted souls, humanly identified with mortal egos, repeatedly indulge their erroneous ways of living, which then become firmly entrenched in the brain as bad habits of mortal behavior.

When Jesus said that men love darkness rather than light, he was referring to the fact that material habits keep millions away from God. He did not mean that all men love darkness—only those who make no effort to resist the temptations of Satan, taking instead the easy way of rolling down the hill of bad habits and thus becoming inured to the darkness of worldly consciousness. Because they shut out the voice of Christ Consciousness whispering in their personal conscience, they shun the infinitely more tempting experience of joy to be had through the good habits urged by the guiding wisdom-light in their souls.

❖ ❖ ❖

Thus Jesus' emphasis that by the light of soul-awakening, the mortal habit of preferring the delusive darkness of materiality can be dispelled from man's consciousness. With repeated acts of will power to meditate regularly and deeply, one attains the supremely satisfying Bliss-contact of God and can recall that joy to his consciousness anytime, anywhere.

❖ ❖ ❖

As long as a person is intoxicated with evil thoughts and ways, his dark mentality will hate the light of truth. The one good thing about bad habits, however, is that they seldom keep their promises. They are eventually found out to be inveterate liars. That is why souls cannot

The "Single" or Spiritual Eye

"The light of the body is the eye: if therefore thine eye be single, thy whole body shall be full of light. But if thine eye be evil, thy whole body shall be full of darkness. If therefore the light that is in thee be darkness, how great is that darkness!" (Matthew 6:22–23).

The God-revealing light in the body is the single eye in the middle of the forehead, seen in deep meditation—the doorway into the presence of God. When the devotee can perceive through this spiritual eye, he beholds his whole body as well as his cosmic body filled with God's light emanating from cosmic vibration.

By fixing the vision of the two eyes at the point between the eyebrows in the interiorized concentration of meditation, one can focus the positive-negative optical energies of the right and left eyes and unite their currents in the single eye of divine light. The ignorant, material man knows nothing of this light. But anyone who has practiced even a little meditation may occasionally see it. When the devotee is further advanced, he sees this light at will, with closed or open eyes, in the daylight or in darkness. The highly developed devotee can behold this light as long as he so desires; and when his consciousness can penetrate into that light, he enters the highest states of transcendent realization.

But when one's gaze and mind are turned away from God and concentrated on evil motives and material actions, his life is filled with the darkness of delusion's ignorance, spiritual indifference, and misery-making habits. The inner cosmic light and wisdom remain hidden. "How great is that darkness" of the material man that he knows little or not at all of divine reality, accepting with glee or resentment whatever offerings of delusion come his way. To live in such dank ignorance is no valid life for the incarnate soul consciousness.

The spiritualized man—his body and mind inwardly illumined with astral light and wisdom, the shadows of physical and mental darkness gone, and the whole cosmos seen as filled with God's light, wisdom, and joy—he in whom the light of Self-realization is fully manifest, receives indescribable joy and the unending guidance of divine wisdom.

forever be deceived or enslaved. Though people of bad habits initially recoil from the thought of better living, after they have had enough of evil ways and reach the point of satiety, and have suffered enough from the consequences, they turn for relief toward the wisdom-light of God, despite any entrenched bad habits that must yet be vanquished. If they continually practice ways of living in harmony with Truth, then in that light they come to realize the joy and inner peace brought by self-control and good habits.

"But he that doeth truth cometh to the light, that his deeds may be made manifest, that they are wrought in God."...The divine seeker, trying every day to change something that is not good in his nature, gradually transcends his old habit-bound material ways. His deeds and his very life are re-created, "wrought in God"; he is in truth born anew. Adhering to the good habit of daily scientific meditation, he sees and is baptized in the light of Christ-wisdom, the divine energy of the Holy Ghost, which actually erases the electrical pathways in the brain formed by bad habits of thought and action. His spiritual eye of intuitive perception is opened, bestowing not only unerring guidance on the path of life, but the vision of and entry into God's heavenly kingdom—and ultimately, oneness with His omnipresent consciousness.

PART III

❖◈◈◈❖

JESUS' YOGA OF DIVINE LOVE

Illustration by Heinrich Hofmann

The Sermon on the Mount

CHAPTER 7

The Beatitudes

And he opened his mouth, and taught them, saying, "Blessed are the poor in spirit: for theirs is the kingdom of heaven" (Matthew 5:2–3).

Parallel reference:

And he lifted up his eyes on his disciples, and said, "Blessed be ye poor: for yours is the kingdom of God" (Luke 6:20).

During his teaching, Jesus let loose, through his voice as well as through his eyes, his divine life force and godly vibration to spread over the disciples, making them calmly attuned and magnetized, able to receive through their intuitional understanding of the full measure of his wisdom.

The lyric verses of Jesus that begin "Blessed are…" have become known as The Beatitudes. To beatify is to make supremely happy; beatitude signifies the blessedness, the bliss, of heaven. Jesus here sets forth with power and simplicity a doctrine of moral and spiritual principles that has echoed undiminished down the ages—tenets by which man's life becomes blessed, filled with heavenly bliss.

The word "poor" as used in the first Beatitude signifies wanting in any outer superficial elegance of spiritual wealth. Those who possess true spirituality never make an ostentatious display of it; they rather express quite naturally a humble paucity of ego and its vainglorious trappings. To be "poor in spirit" is to have divested one's inner being, his spirit, of desire for and attachment to material objects, earthly possessions, materially minded friends, selfish human love. Through this purification of inward renunciation, the soul finds that it has ever possessed all riches of the Eternal Kingdom of Wisdom and Bliss, and thenceforth dwells therein in constant communion with God and His saints.

Poverty "in spirit" does not imply that one should necessarily be a pauper, lest deprivation of basic bodily necessities distract one's mind from God. But it certainly means that one should not settle for material acquisitions instead of spiritual opulence. Persons who are materially rich may be poor in inner spiritual development if wealth gorges their senses; while those who are materially "poor" by choice—who have simplified the outer conditions of their life to make time for God—will garner spiritual riches and fulfillment that no treasury of gold could ever buy.

Thus Jesus commended those souls who are poor in spirit, wholly nonattached to personal worldly goals and fortune in deference to seeking God and serving others: "Ye are blessed for your poverty. It will open the gates to the kingdom of all-sufficient God, who will relieve you from material as well as spiritual want throughout eternity. Blessed are you who are in want and seek Him who alone can relieve your deficiencies forever!"

When the spirit of man mentally renounces desire for objects of this world, knowing them to be illusory, perishable, misleading, and unbecoming to the soul, he begins to find true joy in acquiring permanently satisfying soul qualities. In humbly leading a life of outer simplicity and inner renunciation, steeped in the soul's heavenly bliss and wisdom, the devotee ultimately inherits the lost kingdom of immortal blessedness.

❖ ❖ ❖

"Blessed are they that mourn: for they shall be comforted" (Matthew 5:4).

Parallel reference:

"Blessed are ye that weep now: for ye shall laugh" (Luke 6:21).

The pangs of sorrow suffered by the ordinary person arise from mourning the loss of human love or material possessions, or the nonfulfillment of earthly hopes. Jesus was not extolling this negative state of mind, which eclipses psychological happiness and is utterly detrimental to the retention of spiritual bliss obtained by arduous efforts in meditation. He was speaking of that divine melancholy resulting from the awakening consciousness of separation from God, which creates in the soul an insatiable yearning to be reunited with the Eternal Beloved. Those who really mourn for God, who wail incessantly for Him with ever-increasing zeal in meditation, shall find comfort in the revelation of Wisdom-Bliss sent to them by God.

The spiritually negligent children of God endure life's painful traumas with resentful, defeatist resignation instead of effectively soliciting Divine Aid. It is the adorably naughty baby, crying continuously for spiritual knowledge, who at last attracts the response of the Divine Mother. To Her persistent child, the Merciful Mother comes with Her solace of wisdom and love, revealed through intuition or by a glimpse of Her own Presence. No surrogate consolation can assuage instantaneously the bereavement of unnumbered incarnations.

Those whose spiritual mourning is appeased by material fulfillments will find themselves grieving again when those fragile securities are snatched away by the exigencies of life or by death. But those who weep for Truth and God, refusing to be quieted by any lesser offering, will be forever comforted in the arms of Blissful Divinity.

"Blessed are you who cry for God-realization now, for by that single-minded yearning you shall attain. With the entertainment of ever new joy found in divine communion, you shall laugh and rejoice throughout eternity!"

❖ ❖ ❖

"Blessed are the meek: for they shall inherit the earth" (Matthew 5:5).

Humbleness and meekness create in man a bottomless receptacle of recipiency to hold Truth. A proud irascible individual, like the proverbial rolling stone, rolls down the hill of ignorance and gathers no moss of wisdom, while meek souls at peace in the valley of eager mental readiness gather waters of wisdom, flowing from sources human and divine, to nourish their flowering vale of soul qualities.

The imperious egotist is easily riled, defensive, and resentfully offensive, repelling emissaries of wisdom who seek entry into the castle of his life; but the meek and humbly receptive attract the unseen assistance of beneficent angels of cosmic forces proffering material, mental, and spiritual well-being. Thus do the meek of spirit inherit not only all wisdom, but the earth, that is, earthly happiness, along with it.

❖ ❖ ❖

"Blessed are they which do hunger and thirst after righteousness: for they shall be filled" (Matthew 5:6).

Parallel reference:

"Blessed are ye that hunger now: for ye shall be filled" (Luke 6:21).

The words "thirst" and "hunger" provide an apt metaphor for man's spiritual quest. One must first have thirst for the theoretical knowledge of how to attain salvation. After he quenches this thirst by learning the practical technique of actually contacting God, he can then satisfy his inner hunger for Truth by feasting daily on the divine manna of spiritual perception resulting from meditation.

Those who seek appeasement in material things find that their thirst of desires is never slaked, nor is their hunger ever satisfied in the acquirement of possessions. The urge in every man to fill an inner emptiness is the soul's desire for God. It can only be alleviated by realizing one's immortality and imperishable state of divinity in God-union. When man foolishly tries to quench his soul thirst with the substitutes of sense happiness, he gropes from one evanescent pleasure to another, ultimately rejecting them all as inadequate.

Sense pleasures are of the body and lower mind; they bring no nourishment to man's inmost being. Spiritual starvation, suffered by all who would subsist on sense offerings, is allayed only by righteousness—the actions, attitudes, and attributes that are right for the soul: virtue, spiritual behavior, bliss, immortality.

Righteousness means acting rightly in the physical, mental, and spiritual departments of life. Persons who feel a great thirst and hunger for fulfilling the supreme duties of life receive the ever new bliss of God: "Blessed are you who thirst for wisdom and who esteem virtue and righteousness as the real food to appease your inner hunger, for you shall have that lasting happiness brought only by adhering to divine ideals—unparalleled satisfaction of heart and soul."

❖ ❖ ❖

"Blessed are the merciful: for they shall obtain mercy" (Matthew 5:7).

Mercy is a sort of fatherly heartache for the deficiency in an erring child. It is an intrinsic quality of the Divine Nature. The life story of Jesus is replete with accounts of mercy sublimely manifest in his actions and personality. In perfected divine sons of God, we see revealed the hidden transcendent Father as He is. The God of Moses is depicted as a God of wrath (though I do not believe Moses, who spoke to God "face to face, as a man speaketh unto his friend," ever thought of God as the vengeful tyrant portrayed in the Old Testament). But the God of Jesus was so gentle. It was that gentleness and mercy of the Father that Jesus expressed when, instead of judging and destroying the enemies who would crucify him, he asked of the Father to forgive them, "for they know not what they do."

With the patient heart of God, Jesus looked upon humanity as little children who did not understand. If a wee child picks up a knife and strikes you, you do not want to kill that child in retaliation. It does not realize what it has done. When one looks upon humanity as a loving father looks after his children, and is ready to suffer for them that they might receive a little of the sunshine and power of his spirit, then one becomes Christlike: God in action.

The wise alone can be really merciful, for with divine insight they perceive even wrongdoers as souls—God's children who deserve sympathy, forgiveness, help, and guidance when they go astray. Mercy implies the capacity for being helpful; only developed or qualified souls are capable of being practically and mercifully useful. Mercy expresses itself in usefulness when the fatherly heartache tempers the rigidity of exacting judgment and offers not only forgiveness but actual spiritual help in eliminating the error in an individual.

The morally weak but willing-to-be-good, the sinner (he who transgresses against his own happiness by flouting divine laws), the physically decrepit, the mentally impaired, the spiritually ignorant—all need merciful help from souls whose inner development qualifies them to render understanding aid. Jesus' words exhort the devotee: "To receive divine mercy, be merciful to yourself by making yourself spiritually qualified, and be merciful also to other deluded children of God. Persons who continuously develop themselves in every way, and who mercifully feel and alleviate the lack of all-round development in others, surely will melt the heart of God and obtain for themselves His unending and matchlessly helpful mercy."

❖ ❖ ❖

"Blessed are the pure in heart: for they shall see God" (Matthew 5:8).

The consummate religious experience is direct perception of God, for which the purification of the heart is requisite. On this, all scriptures agree. The Bhagavad Gita, India's immortal scripture of Yoga, the science of religion and God-union, speaks of the blessedness and divine perception of one who has attained this inner purification:

The yogi who has completely calmed the mind and controlled the passions and freed them from all impurities, and who is one with Spirit—verily, he has attained supreme blessedness.

With the soul united to Spirit by yoga, with a vision of equality for all things, the yogi beholds his Self (Spirit-united) in all creatures and all creatures in the Spirit.

He who perceives Me everywhere and beholds everything in Me never loses sight of Me, nor do I ever lose sight of him (Bhagavad Gita VI:27, 29–30).

Since ancient times, the *rishis* of India have scrutinized the very core of truth and detailed its practical relevance to man. Patanjali, the renowned sage of the yoga science, begins his *Yoga Sutras* by declaring: *Yoga chitta vritti nirodha*—" *Yoga* (scientific union with God) is the neutralization of the modifications of *chitta* (the inner 'heart' or power of feeling; a comprehensive term for the aggregate of mind-stuff that produces intelligent consciousness)." Both reason and feeling are derived from this inner faculty of intelligent consciousness.

My revered guru, Swami Sri Yukteswar, one of the first in modern times to reveal the unity of Christ's teachings with India's *Sanatana Dharma*, wrote profoundly about how man's spiritual evolution consists of the purification of the heart. From the state in which consciousness is completely deluded by *maya* ("the dark heart"), man progresses through the successive states of the propelled heart, the steady heart, the devoted heart, and ultimately attains the clean heart, in which, Sri Yukteswarji writes, he "becomes able to comprehend the Spiritual Light, Brahma [Spirit], the Real Substance in the universe."*

God is perceived with the sight of the soul. Every soul in its native state is omniscient, beholding God or Truth directly through intuition. Pure reason and pure feeling are both intuitive; but when reason is circumscribed by the intellectuality of the sense-bound mind, and feeling devolves into egoistic emotion, these instrumentalities of the soul produce distorted perceptions.

Restoration of the lost clarity of divine sight is the purport of this Beatitude. The blessedness known to the perfectly pure of heart is none other than that referred to in Saint John's Gospel: "But as many as received him, to them gave he power to become the sons of God." To every devotee who receives and reflects the omnipresent Light Divine, or Christ Consciousness, through a purified transparency of heart and mind, God gives power to reclaim the bliss of divine sonhood, even as did Jesus.

Transparency to Truth is cultivated by freeing the consciousness, the heart's feeling and the mind's reason, from the dualistic influences of attraction and aversion. Reality cannot be accurately reflected in a consciousness ruffled by likes and dislikes, with their restless passions and desires, and the roiling emotions they engender—anger, jealousy, greed, moody sensitivity. But when *chitta*—human knowing and feeling—is calmed by meditation, the ordinarily agitated ego gives way to the blessed calmness of soul perception.

Purity of the intellect gives one the power of correct reasoning, but purity of the heart gives one the contact of God. Intellectuality is a quality of the power of reason, and wisdom is the liberating quality of the soul. When reason is purified by calm discrimination it metamorphoses into wisdom. Pure wisdom and the divine understanding of a pure

---

* See Chapter 3, Sutras 23–32 in *The Holy Science* by Swami Sri Yukteswar (published by Self-Realization Fellowship).

heart are the two sides of the same faculty. Indeed, the purity of heart, or feeling, referred to by Jesus depends on the guidance of all action by discriminative wisdom—the adjusting of human attitudes and behavior by the sacred soul qualities of love, mercy, service, self-control, self-discipline, conscience, and intuition. The pure-eyed vision of wisdom must be combined with the untainted feeling of the heart. Wisdom reveals the righteous path, and the cleansed heart desires and loves to follow that path. All wisdom-revealed soul qualities must be followed wholeheartedly (not merely intellectually or theoretically).

Ordinary man's occluded vision cognizes the gross shells of matter but is blind to the all-pervading Spirit. By the perfect blending of pure discrimination and pure feeling, the penetrating eye of all-revealing intuition is opened, and the devotee gains the true perception of God as present in one's soul and omnipresent in all beings—the Divine Indweller whose nature is a harmonic blend of infinite wisdom and infinite love.

❖ ❖ ❖

"Blessed are the peacemakers: for they shall be called the children of God" (Matthew 5:9).

They are the real peacemakers who generate peace from their devotional practice of daily meditation. Peace is the first manifestation of God's response in meditation. Those who know God as Peace in the inner temple of silence, and who worship that Peace-God therein, are by this relationship of divine communion His true children.

Having felt the nature of God as inner peace, devotees want the Peace-God to be always manifest in their home, in the neighborhood, in the nation, among all nationalities and races. Anyone who brings peace to an inharmonious family has established God there. Anyone who removes the misunderstanding between souls has united them in God's peace. Anyone who, forsaking national greed and selfishness, works to create peace amidst warring nations, is establishing God in the heart of those nations. The initiators and facilitators of peace manifest the unifying Christ-love that identifies a soul as a child of God.

"Son of God" consciousness makes one feel love for all beings. Those who are God's true children cannot feel any difference between an Indian, American, or any other nationality or race. For a little while immortal souls are garbed in white, black, brown, red, or olive-colored bodies. Are people looked upon as variously foreign when they wear different colored clothes? No matter what one's nationality or the color of his body, all of God's children are souls. The Father recognizes no man-made designations; He loves all, and His children must learn to live in that same consciousness. When man confines his identity to his clannish human nature, it gives rise to unending evils and the specter of war.

Human beings have been given potentially limitless power, to prove that they are indeed the children of God. In such technologies as the atomic bomb we see that unless man uses his powers rightly, he will destroy himself. The Lord could incinerate this earth in a second if He lost patience with His erring children, but He doesn't. And as He would never misuse His omnipotence, so we, being made in His image, must also behave like gods and conquer hearts with the power of love, or humanity as we know it will surely perish. Man's power to make war is increasing; so must his ability to make peace. The best deterrent against the threat of war is brotherhood, the realization that as God's children we are one family.

Anyone who stirs up strife among brother nations under the guise of patriotism is a traitor to his divine family—a faithless child of God. Anyone who keeps family members, neighbors, or friends fighting through fostering falsehoods and gossip, or who is in any way a maker of disturbance, is a desecrator of God's temple of harmony.

Christ and the great ones have given the recipe for peace within and among individuals and nations. How long man has lived in the darkness of misunderstanding and ignorance of those ideals. The true Christ-method of living can banish human conflicts and the horror of war and bring about peace and understanding on earth; all prejudices and enmities must fall away. That is the challenge placed before those who would be the peacemakers of God.

❖ ❖ ❖

"Blessed are they which are persecuted for righteousness' sake: for theirs is the kingdom of heaven" (Matthew 5:10).

The bliss of God will visit those souls who endure with equanimity the torture of the unjust criticism of so-called friends, as well as enemies, for doing what is right, and who remain uninfluenced by wrong customs or society's harmful habits. A devotee of righteousness will not bend to social pressure to drink just because he happens to be at a gathering where cocktails are served, even when others mock him for nonparticipation in their pleasure. Moral rectitude brings short-term ridicule but long-term rejoicing, for persistence in self-control yields bliss and perfection. An eternal kingdom of heavenly joy, to enjoy in this life and the beyond, is earned by those who live and die in right behavior.

Worldly people who prefer sensory indulgences to God-contact are truly the foolish ones, because by ignoring what is right, and therefore good for them, they will have to reap the consequences. The righteous devotee pursues that which is beneficial for him in the highest sense. One who relinquishes the desultory ways of the world and cheerfully stands the scorn of shortsighted friends for his idealism demonstrates that he is fit for the unending bliss of God.

The above verse also offers encouragement to those who are persecuted and tortured by sensory temptations and bad habits when they have resolved to cling to moral ideals and spiritual practices. They are righteous indeed, following the right way of self-control and meditation, which will in time defeat temptations and win the kingdom of eternal joy for the victorious.

No matter how powerful temptations are, or how strong bad habits, they can be resisted with the wisdom-guided power of self-control and by holding to the conviction that no matter what pleasure is promised by temptation, it will always give sorrow in the end. The irresolute inevitably become hypocrites, justifying wrong behavior while succumbing to the wiles of temptation. The honey of God, though sealed in mystery, is what the soul truly craves. Those who meditate with undaunted patience and persistence break the mystery seal, and uninhibitedly imbibe the heavenly nectar of immortality.

Heaven is that state of transcendental, omnipresent joy where no sorrows ever dare to tread. By steadfast righteousness, the devotee will ultimately reach that beatific bliss from which there is no fall. Vacillating devotees, not fixed in meditation, can slip from this supernal happiness; but those who are resolute gain that blessedness permanently. The kingdom of Cosmic Consciousness is owned by the King of Heavenly Bliss, and by the elevated souls who are merged in Him. Hence it is said of devotees who unite their ego with God, becoming one with the King of the Universe: "Theirs is the kingdom of heaven."

❖ ❖ ❖

"Blessed are ye, when men shall revile you, and persecute you, and shall say all manner of evil against you falsely, for my sake.

"Rejoice, and be exceeding glad: for great is your reward in heaven: for so persecuted they the prophets which were before you" (Matthew 5:11–12).

Parallel reference:

"Blessed are ye, when men shall hate you, and when they shall separate you from their company, and shall reproach you, and cast out your name as evil, for the Son of man's sake.

"Rejoice ye in that day, and leap for joy: for, behold, your reward is great in heaven: for in the like manner did their fathers unto the prophets" (Luke 6:22–23).

The foregoing verses do not require one to conscript a band of revilers to make one fit for the kingdom of heaven. In spite of one's best efforts for good in the world and in oneself, the barbs of persecutors will never be absent, as Jesus well knew. The ornery nature of the ego makes the undisciplined man uncomfortable and mean-spirited toward those who are morally or spiritually different from himself. The goadings of satanic divisive delusion keep the self-appointed critic ever scanning for reasons to malign others. Jesus encouraged his followers not to be dismayed or intimidated if in trying to live spiritually they find that materially minded persons do not understand. Those who can pass through the test of scorn cheerfully, and without yielding to wrong ways in order to "fit in," will gain the happiness that results from clinging to virtuous bliss-yielding habits.

It should be considered no great loss when the reproachers and haters and defamers "shall separate you from their company." Actually, persons who are thus shunned are blessed that by such ostracism their souls are kept away from the bad influence of the company of nonunderstanding, misbehaving persons.

The spiritually dedicated should never become despondent, no matter how people speak evil against them or vilify their good name in declarations of wrongdoing. Blessed are those whose name is denigrated for not cooperating with worldly or evil ways, for their names shall be engraved in the silently admiring heart of God.

The Bhagavad Gita (XII:18–19) similarly expresses the Lord's regard for such devotees: "He who is tranquil before friend and foe alike, and in encountering adoration and insult, and during the experiences of warmth and chill and of pleasure and suffering; who has relinquished attachment, regarding blame and praise in the same light; who is quiet and easily contented, not attached to domesticity, and of calm disposition and devotional—that person is dear to Me."

One must follow what one knows to be right, in spite of criticism. Everyone should honestly, without egotistical bias, analyze himself; and if he is right, he should hold to his joy-producing righteous actions uninfluenced by either praise or blame. But if one is wrong, he should be glad of the opportunity to correct himself and thus remove one more obstacle to lasting happiness. Even unjust criticism will make the disciple purer than ever and enthuse him all the more to follow the ways of inner peace instead of yielding to temptations urged by bad company.

It is in the company of God that one remains blessed. One has to find time for Him in the peace of meditation. Why waste all of one's leisure hours in frequenting the movies or watching television, or in other idle pastimes? In cultivating and adhering to divine habits, the devotee finds true impetus to rejoice in his inner contentment and in knowing he will ultimately inherit the kingdom of eternal fulfillment.

The devotee who is denounced for holding to spiritual ways should not flatter himself that being persecuted for God's sake means he is doing the Lord some great favor. "To be persecuted for my sake" or "for the Son of man's sake," signifies being chastised for holding to those practices the devotee has undertaken at the behest of his Christlike guru for the sake of acquiring attunement with God.

Jesus spoke to his disciples and followers as their God-sent guru or savior: "Blessed are you when for following the Son of man (the Christlike guru-preceptor, the representative of God) you are criticized and belittled for preferring to walk in the light of his God-tuned wisdom instead of stumbling with the masses along worldly paths of darkness and ignorance."

To be hated, ostracized, reproached, or cast out is in itself no cause for blessing if one is morally or spiritually degenerate; but when despite persecution the devotee clings to truth as manifested in the life and teachings of a Christlike guru, then he will be free in everlasting blessedness. "Rejoice ye in that day, and feel the uplifting holy vibration of ever new joy; for behold, those who will toil and labor and accept pain to follow the divine way will be rewarded in heaven with eternal bliss.

"Those who persecute you are a continuity of the successive generations of those who persecuted the prophets. Think to what great evil those forefathers came, and consider what reward in heaven the prophets received from God for bearing the persecution from ignorant persons for His name's sake. Holding on to spiritual principles, even if one has to lose his body as did the martyrs of yore, brings the reward of divine inheritance of God's kingdom of Everlasting Exultation."

"Great is your reward in heaven" signifies the state of eternal bliss felt in stabilizing the divine contact of God experienced in meditation: One who performs elevating good actions on earth will, according to the law of karma, reap the fruits of those deeds either in the inner heaven on earth while living, or in the supernal heavenly realms after death.

One's store of good karma and spiritual tenacity determines one's heavenly reward in life or in the afterlife. Advanced souls, those who by meditation are able to experience the ever-newly joyous state of Self-realization, and who can remain constantly in that inner heavenly bliss where God dwells, carry with them a portable heaven wherever they go. The astral sun of the spiritual eye begins to reveal to their consciousness the astral heaven wherein reside, in graduated spheres, virtuous souls and saints, liberated beings and angels. Gradually, the light of the spiritual eye opens its portals, drawing the consciousness into progressively higher spheres of Heaven: the omnipresent golden aura of the Holy Ghost Cosmic Vibration in which are enfolded the mysteries of the finer forces that inform all regions of vibratory existence (wherein is found the "pearly gate" or entryway into the astral heaven through its pearl-like rainbow-hued firmament, or boundary wall); the Christ Heaven of God's reflected Consciousness shining His intelligence on the vibratory realm of creation; and the ultimate heaven of Cosmic Consciousness, the everlasting, immutably blissful transcendental Kingdom of God.

Only those souls who can keep their consciousness fixed in the spiritual eye during earthly existence, even during trials and persecutions, will in this life or the afterlife enter the blissful states of the higher regions of Heaven where the most extraordinary advanced souls dwell in the delightful proximity of God's all-freeing presence.

Though Jesus cites especially the great reward accruing to advanced souls, even a lesser measure of blissful God-communion will bring a commensurate heavenly reward. Those who make some progress and then compromise their spiritual ideals or give up meditating, because they feel inwardly persecuted by the effort required or are outwardly discouraged by worldly influences or by the criticism of relatives, neighbors, or so-called friends, lose the contact of heavenly bliss. But those who are divinely stalwart not only retain the bliss they acquire by meditation but are doubly rewarded, finding their stability giving rise to ever greater fulfillment. This is the psychological heavenly reward resulting from applying the law of habit: Anyone who becomes fixed in inner bliss by meditation will be rewarded with ever-increasing joy that will remain with him even when he leaves this earthly plane.

The heavenly state of meditative bliss felt in this life is a foretaste of the ever new joy felt in the immortalized soul in the after-death state. The soul carries that joy into the sublime astral regions of celestial beauty, where lifetronic blossoms unfold their rainbow petals in the garden of ether, and where the climate, atmosphere, food, and inhabitants are made of different vibrations of multihued light—a kingdom of refined manifestations more in harmony with the essence of the soul than are the crudities of the earth.

Righteous people who resist temptation on earth, but who do not totally free themselves from delusion, are rewarded after death with a rejuvenating rest in this astral heaven among the many half-angels and half-redeemed souls who carry on a life that is exceedingly superior to that on earth. There they enjoy the results of their good astral karma for a karmically predetermined span; after which time, their remaining earthly karma pulls them back into reincarnation in a physical body. Their "great reward" in the astral heaven enables them to manifest desired conditions at will, dealing entirely with vibrations and energy, not with the fixed properties of solids, liquids, and gaseous substances encountered during the earthly sojourn. In the astral heaven, all furnishings, properties, climatic conditions, and transportation are subject to the astral beings' will power, which can materialize, manipulate, and dematerialize the lifetronic substance of that finer world according to preference.

Completely redeemed souls harbor no mortal desires in their hearts when they leave the shores of the earth. These souls become permanently fixed as pillars in the mansion of Cosmic Consciousness, and never again reincarnate on the earth plane, unless they do so willingly in order to bring earthbound souls back to God.*

Such are God's prophets: souls who are anchored in Truth and return to earth at the command of God to lead others to spiritual ways by their exemplary conduct and message of salvation. The spiritual state of a prophet or savior is one of complete union with God, which qualifies him to declare God in the mysterious spiritual way. They are usually extraordinary reformers who show to mankind extraordinary spiritual examples. They demonstrate the power and superior influence of love over hate, wisdom over ignorance, even if it means martyrdom. They refuse to give up their truths no matter the degree of physical or mental persecution, dishonor, or false accusations; and just as steadfastly, they refuse to hate their persecutors or to use the expediency of revenge to

---

* "Him that overcometh will I make a pillar in the temple of my God, and he shall go no more out" (Revelation 3:12).

quell their enemies. They demonstrate and retain the restraint and for-
bearance of God's all-forgiving love, being themselves sheltered in that
Infinite Grace.

In all the great ones—those who come on earth to show to humanity the way to everlasting blessedness or bliss consciousness—are found
the godly traits extolled by Jesus as the way to beatitude. In the Bhagavad Gita, Sri Krishna enumerates comprehensively these requisite soul
qualities that distinguish the divine man:

*(The sage is marked by) humility, lack of hypocrisy, harmless-
ness, forgivingness, uprightness, service to the guru, purity of
mind and body, steadfastness, self-control;*

*Indifference to sense objects, absence of egotism, under-
standing of the pain and evils (inherent in mortal life): birth,
illness, old age, and death;*

*Nonattachment, nonidentification of the Self with such as
one's children, wife, and home; constant equal-mindedness in
desirable and undesirable circumstances;*

*Unswerving devotion to Me by the yoga of nonseparative-
ness, resort to solitary places, avoidance of the company of
worldly men;*

*Perseverance in Self-knowledge; and meditative percep-
tion of the object of all learning—the true essence or meaning
therein. All these qualities constitute wisdom; qualities opposed
to them constitute ignorance (Bhagavad Gita XIII:7–11).*

By cultivation of the above virtues, then even in this material world
man can live in the beatific consciousness of the soul, a true child of God.
He makes his own life, and many of those he contacts, radiant with the
infinite light, joy, and love of the Eternal Father.

CHAPTER 8

Divine Love:
Highest Goal of Religion and of Life

And, behold, a certain lawyer stood up, and tempted him, saying, "Master, what shall I do to inherit eternal life?"

He said unto him, "What is written in the law? How readest thou?"

And he answering said, "Thou shalt love the Lord thy God with all thy heart, and with all thy soul, and with all thy strength, and with all thy mind; and thy neighbour as thyself."

And he said unto him, "Thou hast answered right: this do, and thou shalt live" (Luke 10:25–28).

Parallel passage from Gospel of Mark:

And one of the scribes came, and having heard them reasoning together, and perceiving that he had answered them well, asked him, "Which is the first commandment of them all?"

And Jesus answered him, "The first of all the commandments is, 'Hear, O Israel; The Lord our God is one Lord: And thou shalt love the Lord thy God with all thy heart, and with all thy soul, and with all thy mind, and with all thy strength': this is the first commandment. And the second is like, namely this, 'Thou shalt love thy neighbour as thyself.' There is none other commandment greater than these" (Mark 12:28–31).

The whole purpose of religion—indeed, of life itself—is encapsulated in the two paramount commandments cited by Lord Jesus in these verses. In them lies the essence of eternal truth distinguishing all bona fide spiritual paths, the irreducible imperative that man must embrace as an individualized soul separated from God if he would reclaim the realization of oneness with his Maker.

"This do, and thou shalt live," Jesus told the lawyer who had asked how to obtain eternal life. That is: "If you can love God wholly in actual communion in daily meditation, and show by your actions your love for your neighbor (your divine brother) even as you love yourself, you will rise above the mortal consciousness of this delusive plane of life and death and realize the eternal changeless Spirit existing within yourself and in Its everywhereness."

"On these two commandments hang all the law and the prophets," proclaimed Jesus to the lawyer mentioned in Matthew. And to the scribe in Mark who asked which divine commandment was preeminent, Jesus answered: "The Cosmic Sovereign and our Protector, our one God, is the sole Lord and Master of all creation. He created you as one of His children, made in His image and bearing the divine relation ordained by Him. It behooves you to love spontaneously your Creator with the love He implanted in you—with all the divine love in your heart, with all the intuitive perception of your soul, with all the attention of your mind, and with all the strength of your mental determination and physical energy."

This, Jesus declared, is the foremost of all cosmic laws ordained by the Spirit for soul upliftment and liberation; for through the portal of man's love God enters into oneness with him, a union that liberates him from the bondage of delusion. To love God supremely is to receive from Him eternal contentment and fulfillment, with freedom from all human desires that irresponsibly provoke continuous births and deaths with their unforeseen miseries.

Jesus praised the understanding demonstrated by the scribe, and assured him that he was near to attaining a high degree of spiritual consciousness, because this man realized that to love God in His supremacy and in His innate intimacy in all beings is "more than all whole burnt offerings and sacrifices." To worship the Creator through outward religious formalities is to maintain a separateness between the worshiper and Worshiped; but to love Him is to become His friend, His son, and one with Him.

For God to command that man love Him above everything else might seem unbecoming of an all-powerful Deity. But all avatars and saints have known in their hearts that this is not to appease some quixotic whim of God, but is rather a necessity through which the individualized soul can make a conscious connection with its Source. God can live without man's love; but as the wave cannot live without the ocean, so it is not possible for man to exist without the love of God. The thirst for love in every human heart is because man is made in God's image of love. So the avatars and saints call upon mankind to love God, not because of compulsion or commandment, but because the ocean of His love surges behind the little wave of love in every heart.

A great saint of India said: "He is the cleverest who wholeheartedly seeks God first"; for in finding Him, he receives, along with Him, everything that is of God. To love God is to contact creation's Munificent Provenance. Many a worldly man foolishly engages his heart, mind, soul, and physical strength in the pursuit of money or human love or earthly power, only to lose them—if perchance he had found them—at the time of death. The wisest use of life is to invest it in seeking God, the one treasure that satisfies forever and can never be lost or diminished.

Though one must love God in order to know Him, it is equally true that one must know God in order to love Him. No one can love anything of which he is entirely ignorant; no one can love a person who is completely unknown to him. But those who meditate deeply do "know," because they find proof of the existence of God as the ever new Joy felt in meditation, or the Cosmic Sound of *Aum* (Amen) heard in deep silence, or the Cosmic Love experienced while concentrating devotion in the heart, or the Cosmic Wisdom that dawns as inner enlightenment, or the Cosmic Light evoking visions of Infinity, or the Cosmic Life felt during meditation when the little life is joined to the greater Life in everything.

Any devotee who even once has sensed God as any one of His tangible manifestations in meditation cannot help but love Him when thus touched by His thrilling qualities. Most people never really love God because they little know how lovable the Lord is when He visits the heart of the meditating devotee. This actual contact of the transcendental presence of God is possible to determined devotees who persist in meditation and continuous soulful prayers.

There is but one Originator of all capabilities of man: God is the Creator of our love with which we love, of our souls with which we claim immortality, of our minds and mental processes with which we think and reason and accomplish, of our vitality with which we engage in the activities of life. We should use all these gifts in a supreme energetic effort in meditation to express our love to God until we feel consciously His responding manifestation.

The average religionist rationalizes the fulfillment of his spiritual obligation through absentminded prayers or mechanical rituals, or circuitous wanderings in the forest of theology and dogma. He may attempt to feel love and devotion for God in his heart, and to put his mind on God as best he can during times of prayer; and he may try to love God "with all his strength" by vigorously singing, dancing, or even rolling on the ground as do some sects of "Holy Rollers." When it comes to loving God with all his soul he is at a loss, as he does not even know what the soul is. The only time he knows something of his soul (and then only in an unconscious way) is in deep, dreamless sleep. In that state, the "strength" or life energy is switched off from the five senses and withdrawn inward; the consciousness of oneself as a physical being is gone. At night human beings have a glimpse of their real Self, the soul; each morning upon awakening the majority again take up their mistaken identity as a mortal man or woman.

Outward attempts to apply Jesus' teaching usually yield only minimal external satisfaction, not God-realization. But there is an inner meaning to the exhortation to love God with all one's heart, mind, soul, and strength. Jesus used these simple scriptural terms, but projected his understanding that in them is the whole science of yoga, the transcendental way of divine union through meditation. In India, where spiritual understanding had developed for thousands of years before the time of Jesus, God-knowing sages elaborated these concepts as a comprehensive spiritual philosophy to guide devotees systematically on the path to liberation. When a person makes the effort in meditation to know God, using the sincerity of his heart and deepest feelings, and the intuition of his soul, and all the powers of concentration of his mind, and all his interiorized life energy, or strength, he will surely succeed.

That system of spiritual culture whereby one learns to "love God with all your heart" is known in India as *Bhakti Yoga*—union with

God through unconditional love and devotion. The *bhakta* realizes that whatever is in a person's heart, that is where his concentration is—on the thing he loves. As the lover's heart is on the beloved and the drunkard's is on his drink, so the devotee's heart is continuously absorbed in love for his Divine Beloved.

To "love God with all your mind" means with focused concentration. India has specialized in the science of concentrating the mind one-pointedly through definite techniques, so that during the time of worship the devotee is able to keep his whole attention on God. If while offering prayerful devotions the mind is constantly flitting to thoughts of work or food or bodily sensations or other diversions, that is not loving God with all the mind. The Bible teaches: "Pray without ceasing"; India's yoga science gives the actual methodology to worship God with that fully concentrated mind.

To "love God with all your soul" means to enter the state of superconscious ecstasy, direct perception of the soul and its oneness with God. When no thoughts cross the mind, but there is a conscious all-knowingness, when one knows through intuitive realization that he can do anything just by so ordering it, then one is in the expanded state of superconsciousness. It is the realization of the soul as the reflection of God, the soul's connection with the consciousness of God. It is a state of exceeding joy: the soul's crystalline perception of the omnipresent Spirit reflected as the joy of meditation.

To love God with all the soul requires the complete stillness of transcendent interiorization. This cannot be achieved while praying aloud, moving the hands this way and that, singing or chanting, or doing anything else that activates the sensory-muscular apparatus of the body. Just as in deep sleep the body and senses become inert, that inner withdrawal is characteristic also of superconscious ecstasy—only ecstasy is much deeper than sleep. Ten million sleeps do not describe the joy of it. That is the state in which one can know the soul, and with that true Self wholly adore Him who is Love itself.

The fulfillment of the divine command to love God with all one's heart, mind, and soul is made possible by the science that enables the devotee to "love God with all thy strength." Yoga teaches that science.

When one sleeps, the conscious mind is inactive; the strength is withdrawn from the sensory-motor apparatus of the brain and from the muscles and nerves and is concentrated in the faculties of the subconscious mind. One cannot go into the sleep state of subconsciousness unless, usually passively, the life force has been switched off from the conscious sensory and motor nervous system; and one cannot go into the superconscious state, transcending the subconsciousness, without consciously switching off the life energy from the senses and muscles.

The mastery of life energy that enables one to love God with all one's strength begins with posture (*asana*, training the body to maintain with ease and without restlessness the correct posture for motionless meditation) and breathing exercises for life-force control (*pranayama*, techniques to quiet the breath and heart). By such practice, the heart becomes quiet, effectively switching off the energy from the senses and stilling the restless breath that keeps man tied to body consciousness. The yogi is able to focus on God without the intrusive pull of the flesh. The mind, disconnected from sensations, becomes transcendentally interiorized (*pratyahara*). The devotee can then use that free mind in a communion of love for God. When the devotee can love God with an inwardly concentrated mind, he begins to feel that love for God in his heart, exquisitely permeating every nuance of his feelings with the presence of God. The God-saturated heart then feels the Beloved Lord in the deepest recesses of the soul where the little love meets and is enfolded by the Great Love. The feeling of God in the soul expands into realization of God in His everywhereness (the *samyama* of yoga: *dharana, dhyana, samadhi*).

Jesus went very deep in teachings that appear on the surface to be simple—much deeper than most people understand. That he taught the entire yoga system, the scientific method of union with God, is evidenced in the Book of Revelation in the mystery of the seven stars and seven churches with their seven angels and seven golden candlesticks. God-realization is attained by opening the "seven seals" of these centers of spiritual perception to attain mastery over all astral powers of life and death through which the soul ascends to liberation.

Jesus emphasized that salvation begins with those practices that enable the devotee truly to love God with the supreme offerings of heart, mind, soul, and strength. In India's greatest scripture of yoga, the Bhaga-vad Gita, the Lord speaks in words that parallel the scriptural command-ment cited by Jesus: "Again listen to My supreme word, the most secret of all. Because thou art dearly loved by Me, I will relate what is beneficial to thee. Absorb thy mind in Me; become My devotee; resign all things to Me; bow down to Me. Thou art dear to Me, so in truth do I promise thee: Thou shalt attain Me!"

❖ ❖ ❖

The First Commandment leads the devotee into observance of the second great spiritual law, "like unto it." As one strives to feel God within, he has also a duty to share his experience of God with his neighbors: "Thou shalt love thy neighbor (all races and creatures anywhere with whom one comes in contact) as thyself (as you love your own soul)—be-cause you see God in everyone." Man's neighbor is the manifestation of his greater Self or God. The soul is a reflection of Spirit, a reflection that is in every being and in the vibratory life of all animate and inanimate cosmic decor. To love parents, relatives, associates, countrymen, all races of the earth, all creatures, flowers, stars, which live in the "neighbor-hood" or range of one's consciousness is to love God in His multifarious tangible manifestations. Those persons yet unable to love God as His subtle expressions in meditation can nurture their love for Him as mani-fested in nature and in all beings they contact or sense in any way.

It is God who becomes the father to protect the child, the mother to love the child unconditionally, and friends to help that incarnate soul without the limitation of familial instincts. It is God who has become the adorned earth with its canopy of stars to amuse His children with wonder. It is He who has become the food and the breath and the sus-taining life functions of the multitude of mortal forms. When God's im-manence penetrates man's understanding, it awakens man to his duty and privilege to worship God templed in himself (through meditation), and templed in all beings and things in the universe (through love of his neighbor in the proximity of his cosmic home).

Even saints who love God in transcendental ecstasy in medita-tion find complete redemption only after they have shared their divine attainment by loving God as manifested in all souls in the omnipresent neighborhood of their soul.

Encouraged by love for God in meditation, one might best begin soul neighborliness by reaching out in helpfulness to persons who are outside one's family, yet are nearer than the world at large. Persons instinctively show preference in giving to their families rather than to strangers; and the idea of "the world" itself is a concept far removed and abstract. But when a person lives just for himself and the select few he chooses to favor as his own, he chokes the expansion of his life, and from the spiritual standpoint he does not live at all. On the contrary, when a person extends his sympathy and caring from the "us four and no more" consciousness to his neighbors and to the world, his little life flows into the greater life of God and becomes the Eternal Life—the second requisite in answer to the question put to Christ by the lawyer, "What shall I do to inherit eternal life?"

Most people live in narrow walls of selfishness, never feeling the throb of the universal life of God. Anyone who lives without knowing that his life comes from the eternal life, who abides a solely material existence, dies and reincarnates forgetful of past lives, has not really lived. His mortal consciousness wandered through delusive dream experiences, but his true Self, the soul, never awoke to express its godly nature and immortality. By contrast, any devotee who by meditation realizes the eternal life behind his mortal life lives forever, never losing his conscious existence at the time of death, or from one incarnation to another, or in the eternity of soul freedom in God.

Saints and sages who fulfill the two preeminent commandments are no longer subservient to the discipline of other commandments, for in loving God in transcendental meditation and as manifested in others, the righteousness in all cosmic laws is honored automatically. In the devotee with God-contact, the Framer of Cosmic Law works as a natural intuitive goodness that keeps him always in harmony with the universal codes of God. Millenniums of darkness gathered around the soul may be dispelled gradually by little flames of observance of numerous rules of conduct. But when, by supreme effort of the heart, mind, and strength, the all-pervading light of God visits the soul, then darkness is no more;

the advent of the Great Light engulfs the flickering illumination of disciplined actions. Therefore, to love God through continuous prayer and meditation, and to love God through physical, mental, and spiritual service to His manifestations in one's universal family of neighbors, is the support and essence of the entirety of other laws of human conduct and liberated lives.

❖ ❖ ❖

A rebirth of loving God and loving one's neighbor as urged by Jesus Christ would bring a spirit of oneness to heal the ills of the world.

Only by fellowship with God will harmony and fellowship come on earth. When one actually perceives the Divine Presence in his own soul, he is inspirited with love for his neighbor—Jew and Christian, Muslim and Hindu—in the consciousness that one's true Self and the Selves of all others are equally soul-reflections of the one infinitely lovable God. Utopian social and political agendas will have little long-lasting benefit until humanity learns the eternal science by which followers of any religion may know God in the oneness of soul and Spirit communion.

To observe the "first commandment," as cited by Jesus, is the centric obligation of human life, subordinating and making servile to it the host of demanding responsibilities man gathers unto himself. Jesus supported the scriptural command to "Honor thy father and mother" but love God supremely. Father, mother, friends, beloved ones, are gifts of God. Love the One Love that hides Himself behind all kindly masks. Love Him first and foremost, or times without numbering He will visit the heart and slip away unrecognized and unwelcomed.

To be with God now is of utmost importance. His love is the only shelter in life and death. Time should be utilized to its best advantage; why shouldn't it be to reclaim oneness with the Creator of this Universe, our Infinite Father?

CHAPTER 9

The Kingdom of God Within You

And when he was demanded of the Pharisees, when the kingdom of God should come, he answered them and said, "The kingdom of God cometh not with observation: Neither shall they say, 'Lo here!' or, 'lo there!' for, behold, the kingdom of God is within you" (Luke 17:20–21).

Jesus addresses man as the perennial seeker of permanent happiness and freedom from all suffering: "The kingdom of God—of eternal, immutable, ever-newly blissful Cosmic Consciousness—is within you. Behold your soul as a reflection of the immortal Spirit, and you will find your Self encompassing the infinite empire of God-love, God-wisdom, God-bliss existing in every particle of vibratory creation and in the vibrationless Transcendental Absolute."

The teachings of Jesus about God's kingdom—sometimes in direct language, sometimes in parables pregnant with metaphysical meaning—may be said to be the core of the entirety of his message. The Gospel records that at the very outset of his public ministry, "Jesus came into Galilee, preaching the gospel of the kingdom of God." His exhortation to "seek ye first the kingdom of God" is at the heart of his Sermon on the Mount. The only prayer he is known to have given his disciples beseeches God, "Thy kingdom come." Again and again he spoke of the kingdom of the Heavenly Father and the method of its attainment:

"Except a man be born of water and of the Spirit, he cannot enter into the kingdom of God."

"Strive to enter in at the strait gate: for many, I say unto you, will seek to enter in, and shall not be able."

"No man hath ascended up to heaven, but he that came down from heaven, even the Son of man which is in heaven. And as Moses lifted up the serpent in the wilderness, even so must the Son of man be lifted up."

"And if thine eye offend thee, pluck it out: it is better for thee to enter into the kingdom of God with one eye, than having two eyes to be cast into hell fire."

"I am the door: by me if any man enter in, he shall be saved, and shall go in and out, and find pasture."

"I am the way, the truth, and the life: no man cometh unto the Father, but by me." *

Taken together, these and Jesus' other declarations about the kingdom of God provide for a comprehensive understanding of the simple statement in the present verses that God's kingdom is to be found not by "observation"—use of the matter-tuned senses of sight, hearing, taste, smell, and touch—but by interiorization of the consciousness to perceive the Divine Reality "within you."

"The kingdom of God does not come in response to sensory observation; neither can they find it who say, 'Behold, it is here or there somewhere in the clouds.' Rather, concentrate within and you will find the sphere of God-consciousness hidden behind your material consciousness."

Many people think of heaven as a physical location, a point of space far above the atmosphere and beyond the stars. Others interpret Jesus' statements about the advent of the kingdom of God as referring to the coming of a Messiah to establish and rule over a divine kingdom on earth. In fact, the kingdom of God and the kingdom of heaven consist, respectively, of the transcendental infinitudes of Cosmic Consciousness and the heavenly causal and astral realms of vibratory creation that are considerably finer and more harmonized with God's will than those physical vibrations clustered together as planets, air, and earthly surroundings.

Material objects cognized as sensations of sight, hearing, smell, taste, and touch are constituted of a play of forces originating and existing beyond the observational capabilities of human consciousness. The incipient origin of all material forms and material vibrations lies in

---

* The deeper metaphysical meaning of all these verses, and their application to the science of yoga, is explained comprehensively in *The Second Coming of Christ: The Resurrection of the Christ Within You.*

Cosmic Consciousness. Matter is condensed physical energy; physical energy is condensed astral energy; and astral energy is condensed prototypic thought force of God. Hence Cosmic Consciousness lies hidden within and behind the layers of matter, physical energy, astral energy, and thought or consciousness.

As in the macrocosm, so in the microcosm of the human body: Cosmic Consciousness, which is marked by ever new joy and immortality, is the creator of human consciousness and as such lies within it. From the infinite Cosmic Consciousness, individual souls were conceived; these individualized ideations of the thought of God were cloaked in two further layers of external manifestation by condensation of magnetic causal forces of consciousness into the astral body of luminous life energy and the mortal body of flesh and blood.

Thus the kingdom of God is not separate from the kingdom of matter, but is both within it—pervading it in subtle form as its origin and sustainer—and beyond it, existing in the infinite mansions of the Father beyond the circumscribed physical cosmos.*

That is why Jesus said it is futile to look for heaven with the consciousness concentrated on material vibrations—identified with bodily sensations and pleasures and earthly comforts. In the kingdom of matter and body consciousness man finds disease and mental and physical suffering; but turning within to the inner kingdom he finds the Comforter, the Holy Ghost or Cosmic Vibration of *Aum,* manifesting in the subtle cerebrospinal centers of spiritual consciousness. To be carried along the outgoing stream of material consciousness is to be swept willy-nilly into the hades of Satan's kingdom—the realm of earthly attachments and

---

* "If those who lead you say, 'Look! the kingdom is in heaven,' then the birds of heaven will precede you. If they say to you, 'It is in the sea,' then the fish will precede you. But the kingdom is within you and it is outside of you. If you will know yourselves, then you will be known, and you will realize that you are children of the living Father. But if you do not know yourselves, then you dwell in poverty and you are poverty" (The Gospel of Thomas, verse 3).

His disciples said to him, "…When will the new world come?" He said to them, "What you are looking forward to has come, but you don't know it" (The Gospel of Thomas, verse 51).

Jesus' disciples said unto him: "When will the kingdom come?" Jesus answered, "It will not come by waiting for it. People will not say, 'Look! Here it is!' or 'There it is!' But the kingdom of the Father is spread out upon the earth and people do not see it" (The Gospel of Thomas, verse 113). *(Publisher's Note)*

limitations of the mortal body; to follow the inwardly flowing stream of consciousness by meditating on *Aum* is to reach the blissful kingdom of God that exists behind the opaque obstruction of the physical being.*

Communion with the holy Comforter brings attunement with Christ Consciousness indwelling in the body as the ever perfect soul. Through deeper communion with the Christ Consciousness comes realization of the soul's oneness with omnipresent Spirit—the little Self expanding to its infinite Self to encompass the boundless divine kingdom of ever-existing, ever-conscious, ever-new Bliss.

For every body-circumscribed soul the kingdom of God awaits discovery by those who delve within in meditation to transcend human consciousness and reach the successively higher states of superconsciousness, Christ Consciousness, and Cosmic Consciousness. Those who meditate deeply, concentrating intensely within their state of silence, or neutralized thoughts, withdraw their minds from material objects of sight, sound, smell, taste, and touch—from all bodily sensations and disturbing mental restlessness. In this focused stillness within, they find an ineffable sense of peace. Peace is the first glimpse of the inner kingdom of God.

Devotees who at will can thus interiorize their minds and concentrate fully within the resultant peacefulness will definitely find entry into the kingdom of God-consciousness. That realization gradually unfolds itself as omnipresence, omniscience, ever new bliss, and visions of the realms of eternal light in which all liberated souls move in God, materializing or dematerializing themselves at will. No one can enter this heaven of Cosmic Consciousness unless through the gates of devout concentration and meditation he can penetrate his consciousness deeply within himself. That is why Jesus said unequivocally, "The kingdom of God is within

---

* Among the non-canonical Gospels that have survived from the earliest part of the Christian era is a fragmentary manuscript known as "The Dialogue of the Savior," composed around A.D. 150 and lost until the discovery of the Nag Hammadi manuscripts in 1945. The translation in *The Complete Gospels: Annotated Scholar's Version* includes this passage (14:1–4):

Matthew said: "Lord, I wish to see that place of life...where there is no wickedness but only pure light."

The Lord said, "Brother Matthew, you will not be able to see it as long as you bear flesh."

Matthew said: "Lord, even if I will not be able to see it, let me know it."

The Lord said, "Those who have known themselves have seen it." *(Publisher's Note)*

you," that is, within the transcendent states of your soul perceptions.

There is a beautiful accord between the teachings of Jesus Christ to enter the "kingdom of God within you" and the teachings of yoga set forth by Lord Krishna in the Bhagavad Gita to restore King Soul, the reflection of God in man, to its rightful rulership of the bodily kingdom, with full realization of the soul's godly states of consciousness. When man is settled in that inner kingdom of divine consciousness, the awakened intuitive perception of the soul pierces the veils of matter, life energy, and consciousness and uncovers the God-essence in the heart of all things.

He dwells in the world, enveloping all—everywhere, His hands and feet; present on all sides, His eyes and ears, His mouths and heads;

Shining in all the sense faculties, yet transcending the senses; unattached to creation, yet the Mainstay of all; free from the gunas (modes of Nature), yet the Enjoyer of them.

He is within and without all that exists, the animate and the inanimate; near He is, and far; imperceptible because of His subtlety.

He, the Indivisible One, appears as countless beings; He maintains and destroys those forms, then creates them anew.

The Light of All Lights, beyond darkness; Knowledge itself, That which is to be known, the Goal of all learning, He is seated in the hearts of all (Bhagavad Gita XIII:13–17).

Raja Yoga, the royal way of God-union, is the science of actual realization of the kingdom of God that lies within oneself. Through practice of the sacred yoga techniques of interiorization received during initiation from a true guru, one can find that kingdom by awakening the astral and causal centers of life force and consciousness in the spine and brain that are the gateways into the heavenly regions of transcendent consciousness. One who achieves such awakening knows the omnipresent God in His Infinite Nature, and in the purity of one's soul, and even in the delusive cloaks of changeable material forms and forces.

Patanjali, India's foremost ancient exponent of *Raja Yoga*, outlined eight steps to be followed for ascension into the kingdom of God within.

1. *Yama,* moral conduct: abstaining from injury to others, false-hood, stealing, incontinence, and covetousness.

2. *Niyama:* purity of body and mind, contentment in all circum-stances, self-discipline, self-study (contemplation), and devotion to God.

These first two steps yield self-control and mental calmness.

3. *Asana:* disciplining the body so that it can assume and maintain the correct posture for meditation without fatigue or physical and men-tal restlessness.

4. *Pranayama:* techniques of life-force control that calm the heart and breath and remove sensory distractions from the mind.

5. *Pratyahara:* the power of complete mental interiorization and stillness resulting from withdrawal of the mind from the senses.

6. *Dharana:* the power to use the interiorized mind to become one-pointedly concentrated upon God in one of His aspects through which He reveals Himself to the inward perception of the devotee.

7. *Dhyana:* meditation deepened by the intensity of concentration (*dharana*) that gives the conception of the vastness of God, His attributes as manifested in His endless expansion of Cosmic Consciousness.

8. *Samadhi,* union with God: the full realization of the soul's one-ness with Spirit.

All devotees may find the door to the kingdom of God by concentrat-ing on the spiritual eye, the Christ Consciousness center at the point be-tween the eyebrows. Long and deep meditation as taught by a true guru enables one gradually to convert the consciousness of the material body into that of the astral body, and with the awakened faculties of astral perception to intuit deeper and deeper states of consciousness until one reaches oneness with the Source of consciousness. Entering the door of the spiritual eye, one leaves behind all attachments to matter and the physical body and gains access into the interior infinitudes of God's kingdom.

The tissues of the physical body are made up of cells; the tissue of the astral body is composed of lifetrons—intelligent units of light or life energy. When man is in a state of body attachment, characterized by ten-sion or contraction of life energy into atomic components, the lifetrons of the astral body become compacted, circumscribed by identification with the physical form. By metaphysical relaxation, the lifetronic structure begins to expand—the grip of the flesh on one's identity loosens.

By deeper and deeper meditation, the energy frame of the astral self expands beyond the boundaries of the physical body. The lifetronic body, being of a sphere of existence unconfounded by the delusional stricture of the three-dimensional physical world, has the potential to become one with the Cosmic Energy pervading the whole universe. God as Holy Ghost, Holy Vibration, is the Light of Cosmic Energy; man, made in the image of God, is composed of that light. We are that Light compacted; and we are that Light of our Universal Self.

As a first step toward entering the kingdom of God, the devotee should sit still in the correct meditation posture, with erect spine, and tense and relax the body—for by relaxation the consciousness is released from the muscles. The yogi begins with proper deep breathing, inhaling and tensing the whole body, exhaling and relaxing, several times. With each exhalation all muscular tension and motion should be cast away, until a state of bodily stillness is attained. Then, by concentration techniques, restless motion is removed from the mind. In perfect stillness of body and mind, the yogi enjoys the ineffable peace of the presence of the soul. In the body, life is templed; in the mind, light is templed; in the soul, peace is templed. The deeper one goes into the soul the more that peace is felt; that is superconsciousness. When by deeper meditation the devotee expands that awareness of peace and feels his consciousness spreading with it over the universe, that all beings and all creation are swallowed up in that peace, then he is entering into Cosmic Consciousness. He feels that peace everywhere—in the flowers, in every human being, in the atmosphere. He beholds the earth and all worlds floating like bubbles in that ocean of peace.

The inner peace first experienced by the devotee in meditation is his own soul; the vaster peace he feels by going deeper is God. The devotee who experiences unity with everything has established God in the temple of his infinite inner perception.

In the temple of silence, in the temple of peace,
I will meet Thee, I will touch Thee, I will love Thee!
And coax Thee to my altar of peace.

In the temple of *samadhi,* in the temple of bliss,
I will meet Thee, I will touch Thee, I will love Thee!
And coax Thee to my altar of bliss.*

When restless thoughts have been banished, automatically the mind is made into a sacred temple of peace. God intimates Himself in the temple of silence and then in the temple of peace. The devotee first meets Him as peace flowing out of the mental state in which all thoughts have become transformed into pure intuitive feeling. He touches the Lord with his heart's love and feels Him as joy; his pure love entices God to manifest Himself on the altar of the perception of peace. The advancing devotee feels God not only in meditation, but keeps Him always on the altar of peace in his heart.

In the temple of *samadhi,* oneness with the peace that is God's first manifestation in meditation, the devotee finds a state of ever new bliss, a joy that never grows stale. Bliss is a much deeper state than peace. As a mute person drinking nectar imbibes but cannot describe the ambrosial flavor, so the rapture of bliss found in the temple of *samadhi* moves the experiencer to wordless eloquence. That joy alone can satisfy the innate craving of the human heart. In patient, persistent meditation, day after day, year after year, the devotee lovingly demands of his Lord: "Come to me as joy in *samadhi*-oneness, and remain forever in my heart on the altar of bliss!" When in our hearts, in harmony with the hearts of all who love God in the interior temple of silence and bliss, we rejoice in the joy of our one Beloved, that united joy is a vast altar of God.

It is incumbent on man as a soul to practice that inner silence; to find God now. In the use of the senses amid the exigencies of daily life, the devotee holds to the consciousness: "I am sitting on the peace throne of inner silence." In the midst of activity, he remains inwardly recollected: "I am the god of silence sitting on the throne of each action."

---

* From *Cosmic Chants: Spiritualized Songs for Divine Communion* by Paramahansa Yogananda (published by Self-Realization Fellowship).

"Yoga" of the Christian Saints

Paramahansa Yogananda wrote: "A belief in the Holy Ghost is one thing; actual contact with the Holy Ghost is something else! In the past centuries, great saints such as Francis of Assisi and Teresa of Avila knew the art of contacting the Holy Ghost and the Christ Consciousness and the Cosmic Consciousness—the trifold Unity—by the interiorized intensity of pure devotion."

In her masterworks *The Way of Perfection* and *The Interior Castle,* the renowned mystic Saint Teresa of Avila gives a systematic description, from her own personal experience, of the interiorized states of God-communion. These in essence correspond exactly with the progressively higher states of consciousness expounded in India's centuried, universal soul-science of yoga.

The illumined mystic Saint John of the Cross (contemporary and supporter of Teresa of Avila) speaks of his own experiences of God as the Holy Ghost in Stanzas 14 and 15 of his sublime *Spiritual Canticle.* Explaining the symbolism, Saint John describes the "roaring torrents" as "a spiritual sound and voice overpowering all other sounds and voices in the world....

"This voice, or this murmuring sound of the waters, is an overflowing so abundant as to fill the soul with good, and a power so mighty seizing upon it as to seem not only the sound of many waters, but a most loud roaring of thunder. But the voice is a spiritual voice, unattended by material sounds or the pain and torment of them, but rather with majesty, power, might, delight, and glory: it is, as it were, a voice, an infinite interior sound which endows the soul with power and might. The Apostles heard in spirit this voice when the Holy Spirit descended upon them in the sound 'as of a mighty wind,' as we read in the Acts of the Apostles."...

Evelyn Underhill, in *Mysticism* (Part 1, Chapter 4), wrote: "It is one of the many indirect testimonies to the objective reality of mysticism that the stages of this road, the psychology of the spiritual ascent, as described to us by different schools of contemplatives, always present practically the same sequence of states. The 'school for saints' has never found it necessary to bring its curriculum up to date.

"The psychologist finds little difficulty, for instance, in reconciling the 'Degrees of Orison' described by Saint Teresa—Recollection, Quiet, Union, Ecstasy, Rapt, the 'Pain of God,' and the Spiritual Marriage of the soul—with the four forms of contemplation enumerated by Hugh of Saint Victor, or the Sufi's 'Seven Stages' of the soul's ascent to God, which begin in adoration and end in spiritual marriage. Though each wayfarer may choose different landmarks, it is clear from their comparison that the road is one." *(Publisher's Note)*

His equanimity is upset by no unruly feelings: "I am the prince of silence sitting on the throne of poise." His inner Self, at one with eternity, in life and in death rejoices: "I am the king of immortality reigning on the throne of silence. Destruction of the body, delusion's insults to the soul, impositions of restlessness, trials of life—these are but dramas I am acting in and watching as divine entertainment. I may play for a little while; but always, from the inner refuge of my silence, I behold the unfolding script of life with the calm joy of immortality."

If through practice of meditation one keeps knocking on the doors of silence, God will respond: "Come in. I whispered to you through all guises of nature; and now I say to you, I am Joy—the living Fountain of Joy. Bathe in My waters—wash away your habits, cleanse yourself of fears. I dreamed a beautiful dream for you; but, My child, you made of it a nightmare." God wants His children to be no longer prodigal sons, but to play their roles in life as immortals, that when they leave the stage of this earth they can say, "Father, that was a nice entertainment, but now I am ready to come Home."

It is a sin against the divine nature of the Self to think that there is no chance of being happy, to abandon all hope of attaining peace—these must be exposed as psychological errors born of Satan's interference in the human mind. Infinite happiness and peace are always at hand, just behind the screen of man's ignorance. How could it be possible for anyone to be forever barred from the kingdom of God, when that divine realm is right within him? All one has to do is turn from the darkness of evil and follow the light of goodness.

The proximity of happiness is as close as one's own Self; it isn't even a matter of attaining, but only of lifting the soul-shrouding veil of ignorance. The very word "attaining" implies something one wants but does not have—a metaphysical error. Bliss is the irrevocable divine birthright of every soul. Tear away the intrusive veil, and at once there is contact with that happiness supreme. Spirit is happiness. Soul is the pure reflection of Spirit. Body-bound man fails to perceive this because his consciousness is distorted: The lake of his mind is constantly roiled by the incursion of thoughts and emotions. Meditation quiets the waves of feeling (*chitta*) so that God's reflection as the joyous soul is clearly mirrored within.

Most beginners on the path to the inner kingdom of God find that their meditation is entrapped in restlessness. That is Satan's lair. The devotee must escape by perseverance in yoga practice and devotion. "Whenever the fickle and restless mind wanders away—for whatever reason—let the yogi withdraw it from those distractions and return it to the sole control of the Self....Undoubtedly the mind is fickle and unruly; but by yoga practice and by dispassion, O Arjuna, the mind may nevertheless be controlled. This is My word: Yoga is difficult of attainment by the ungoverned man; but he who is self-controlled will, by striving through proper methods, be able to achieve it."

The habit of being inwardly in the calm presence of God must be developed, so that day and night that consciousness will remain steadfast. It is worth the effort; for to live in the consciousness of God is to be done with enslavement to disease, suffering, and fear. Just be with God; that is the be-all and end-all of life. If one resolves never to go to sleep at night without meditating and feeling the Divine Presence, into one's life will come happiness beyond all expectation. Effort is necessary, but that effort will make one a king enthroned in the kingdom of peace and joy. Time spent in the pursuit of extraneous material things is a waste of man's precious opportunities to know God. I am telling you this from my heart: Blessed is he who makes up his mind never to rest until he has found God.

A subsistent inner happiness unconditioned by any external influence is evident proof of the responding presence of God. Progress in divine communion comes only by meditating with regularity and with deep concentration and devotion. Every day's meditation must be deeper than yesterday's. The devotee who makes the divine quest his overriding concern will find in the kingdom of God eternal safety; no tremor of trouble or trials can cross the threshold of his sanctuary of silence wherein naught is allowed ingress but the blissful, all-loving Father-Mother God.

One who finds within himself that "secret place of the most High" becomes suffused with supreme happiness and divine security.* Whether

---

* "He that dwelleth in the secret place of the most High shall abide under the shadow of the Almighty. I will say of the Lord, He is my refuge and my fortress: my God; in Him will I trust....

"There shall no evil befall thee, neither shall any plague come nigh thy dwelling. For He shall

he is mixing with friends or sleeping or working, he keeps that place only for God. With his consciousness centered in the Lord, he finds *maya's* concentric veils suddenly lifting; in joy the devotee sees God playing hide-and-seek with him in the blossoms, and the stars shining with a stronger Light, and the sky smiling with the Infinite. When his eyes are spiritually opened, the devotee beholds, peering at him through the eyes of everyone, the eyes of the Infinite. Behind the kind or unkind voice of everyone he hears the truthful voice of the Infinite. Behind the wise or helter-skelter will of everyone he perceives the constancy of the will of God. Behind all human loves he feels the supreme love of God. What a wonderful existence, when all of God's disguises are cast off and the devotee is face to face with the Infinite, in blissful oneness of divine communion!

Be always intoxicated with the Divine, with the wave of your consciousness ever at rest on the bosom of the Eternal Sea. When one is kicking and splashing about in the water, there is little consciousness of the ocean itself, but of the struggle. But when one lets go and relaxes, the body floats; it feels in its buoyancy the whole sea lapping around it. That is the way the calm devotee feels God, with the whole universe of Divine Happiness rocking gently beneath his consciousness.

God's kingdom is within you; *He* is within you. Just behind your perceptions, just behind your thoughts, just behind your feelings, He is. Every grain of food you eat, every breath you take, is God. You are not living by food or oxygen, but by the Cosmic Word of God. All powers of mind and action that you use are borrowed from God. Think of Him all the time — before you act, while you are engaged in activity, and after activity. In fulfilling your duty to man, remember foremost your duty to God, without whose delegated power no duties are possible. Feel Him behind your senses of sight, hearing, smell, taste, and touch. Feel His energy in the arms, and legs, and feet. Feel Him as life in each exhalation

---

give His angels charge over thee, to keep thee in all thy ways. They shall bear thee up in their hands, lest thou dash thy foot against a stone....

"Because he hath set his love upon Me, therefore will I deliver him:

"I will set him on high, because he hath known My name. He shall call upon Me, and I will answer him: I will be with him in trouble; I will deliver him, and honour him. With long life will I satisfy him, and shew him My salvation" (Psalms 91:1–16).

and inhalation. Feel His power in your will; His wisdom in your brain; His love in your heart. Wherever God's presence is consciously felt, mortal ignorance melts away.

Those who are wise never miss their daily engagement with God in meditation. They make it the consuming goal of their existence to contact Him. All who persist with that sincerity shall enter the kingdom of God in this life; and to abide in that kingdom is to be eternally free.

❖ ❖ ❖

"Ask, and it shall be given you; seek, and ye shall find; knock, and it shall be opened unto you:

"For every one that asketh receiveth; and he that seeketh findeth; and to him that knocketh it shall be opened."

—Matthew 7:7–8

For further exploration of the original teachings of Jesus…

The Second Coming of Christ

The Resurrection of the Christ Within You

By Paramahansa Yogananda

I n this revelatory commentary on the original teachings of Jesus, Paramahansa Yogananda takes the reader on a profoundly enriching journey through the entirety of the four Gospels. Verse by verse, he illumines the universal path to oneness with God taught by Jesus to his immediate disciples but obscured through centuries of misinterpretation.

In addition to the topics presented in *The Yoga of Jesus,* this comprehensive two-volume work includes in-depth discussions on:

❖ Jesus' wish to restore his original teachings to the world
❖ The techniques used by Jesus to effect divine healings
❖ The practical application of Jesus' numerous parables
❖ "Believe on his name": communion with holy Cosmic Vibration
❖ The "heaven" and "hell" experienced in the after-death state
❖ What are the "last judgment" and "Gabriel's trumpet"?
❖ "Thy sins be forgiven": removing the karma of past wrong actions
❖ Jesus' ideals for a spiritually harmonious marriage
❖ True significance of Jesus' words about "the end of the world"
❖ Mary and Martha: balancing material duties with devotional communion
❖ Using faith to resolve minor difficulties as well as to "move mountains"
❖ How Jesus resurrected his physical body and attained immortality

Hardcover, illustrated with 15 full-color prints, 17 sepia duotones
Available from Self-Realization Fellowship or at any bookstore

ABOUT THE AUTHOR

"The ideal of love for God and service to humanity found full expression in the life of Paramahansa Yogananda....Though the major part of his life was spent outside India, still he takes his place among our great saints. His work continues to grow and shine ever more brightly, drawing people everywhere on the path of the pilgrimage of the Spirit."

> *—from a tribute by the Government of India upon issuing a commemorative stamp in Paramahansa Yogananda's honor on the twenty-fifth anniversary of his passing*

Born in India on January 5, 1893, Paramahansa Yogananda devoted his life to helping people of all races and creeds to realize and express more fully in their lives the beauty, nobility, and true divinity of the human spirit.

After graduating from Calcutta University in 1915, Sri Yogananda took formal vows as a monk of India's venerable monastic Swami Order. Two years later, he began his life's work with the founding of a "how-to-live" school—since grown to twenty-one educational institutions throughout India—where traditional academic subjects were offered together with yoga training and instruction in spiritual ideals. In 1920, he was invited to serve as India's delegate to an International Congress of Religious Liberals in Boston. His address to the Congress and subsequent lectures on the East Coast were enthusiastically received, and in 1924 he embarked on a cross-continental speaking tour.

Over the next three decades, Paramahansa Yogananda contributed in far-reaching ways to a greater awareness and appreciation in the West of the spiritual wisdom of the East. In Los Angeles, he established an international headquarters for Self-Realization Fellowship—the nonsectarian religious society he had founded in 1920. Through his writings, extensive lecture tours, and the creation of numerous Self-Realization Fellowship temples and meditation centers, he introduced thousands of truth-seekers to the ancient science and philosophy of Yoga and its universally applicable methods of meditation.

115

Today, the spiritual and humanitarian work begun by Paramahansa Yogananda continues under the direction of Sri Mrinalini Mata, one of his closest disciples and current president of Self-Realization Fellowship/ Yogoda Satsanga Society of India. In addition to publishing his lectures, writings, and informal talks (including a comprehensive series of lessons for home study), the society also oversees its temples, retreats, and centers around the world; the monastic communities of the Self-Realization Order; and a Worldwide Prayer Circle.

In an article on Sri Yogananda's life and work, Dr. Quincy Howe, Jr., Professor of Ancient Languages at Scripps College, wrote: "Paramahansa Yogananda brought to the West not only India's perennial promise of God-realization, but also a practical method by which spiritual aspirants from all walks of life may progress rapidly toward that goal. Originally appreciated in the West only on the most lofty and abstract level, the spiritual legacy of India is now accessible as practice and experience to all who aspire to know God, not in the beyond, but in the here and now....Yogananda has placed within the reach of all the most exalted methods of contemplation."

The life and teachings of Paramahansa Yogananda are described in his *Autobiography of a Yogi* (see page 120).

Paramahansa Yogananda:
A Yogi in Life and Death

Paramahansa Yogananda entered *mahasamadhi* (a yogi's final conscious exit from the body) in Los Angeles, California, on March 7, 1952, after concluding his speech at a banquet held in honor of H. E. Binay R. Sen, Ambassador of India.

The great world teacher demonstrated the value of yoga (scientific techniques for God-realization) not only in life but in death. Weeks after his departure his unchanged face shone with the divine luster of incorruptibility.

Mr. Harry T. Rowe, Los Angeles Mortuary Director, Forest Lawn Memorial-Park (in which the body of the great master is temporarily placed), sent Self-Realization Fellowship a notarized letter from which the following extracts are taken:

"The absence of any visual signs of decay in the dead body of Paramahansa Yogananda offers the most extraordinary case in our experience....No physical disintegration was visible in his body even twenty days after death.... No indication of mold was visible on his skin, and no visible desiccation (drying up) took place in the bodily tissues. This state of perfect preservation of a body is, so far as we know from mortuary annals, an unparalleled one....At the time of receiving Yogananda's body, the Mortuary personnel expected to observe, through the glass lid of the casket, the usual progressive signs of bodily decay. Our astonishment increased as day followed day without bringing any visible change in the body under observation. Yogananda's body was apparently in a phenomenal state of immutability....

"No odor of decay emanated from his body at any time....The physical appearance of Yogananda on March 27th, just before the bronze cover of the casket was put into position, was the same as it had been on March 7th. He looked on March 27th as fresh and as unravaged by decay as he had looked on the night of his death. On March 27th there was no reason to say that his body had suffered any visible physical disintegration at all. For these reasons we state again that the case of Paramahansa Yogananda is unique in our experience."

ADDITIONAL RESOURCES ON THE KRIYA YOGA TEACHINGS OF PARAMAHANSA YOGANANDA

Self-Realization Fellowship is dedicated to freely assisting seekers worldwide. For information regarding our annual series of public lectures and classes, meditation and inspirational services at our temples and centers around the world, a schedule of retreats, and other activities, we invite you to visit our website or our International Headquarters:

www.yogananda-srf.org

Self-Realization Fellowship
3880 San Rafael Avenue
Los Angeles, CA 90065
(323) 225-2471

SELF-REALIZATION FELLOWSHIP LESSONS

Personal guidance and instruction from Paramahansa Yogananda on the techniques of yoga meditation and principles of spiritual living

If you feel drawn to the spiritual truths described in *The Yoga of Jesus,* we invite you to enroll in the *Self-Realization Fellowship Lessons.*

Paramahansa Yogananda originated this home-study series to provide sincere seekers the opportunity to learn and practice the ancient yoga meditation techniques that he brought to the West—including the science of *Kriya Yoga.* The *Lessons* also present his practical guidance for attaining balanced physical, mental, and spiritual well-being.

The *Self-Realization Fellowship Lessons* are available at a nominal fee (to cover printing and postage costs). All students are freely given personal guidance in their practice by Self-Realization Fellowship monks and nuns.

For more information...

Complete details about the *Self-Realization Fellowship Lessons* are included in the free booklet *Undreamed-of Possibilities.* To receive a copy of this booklet and an application form, please visit our website or contact our International Headquarters.

Also published by Self-Realization Fellowship...

AUTOBIOGRAPHY OF A YOGI

By Paramahansa Yogananda

This acclaimed autobiography presents a fascinating portrait of one of the great spiritual figures of our time. With engaging candor, eloquence, and wit, Paramahansa Yogananda narrates the inspiring chronicle of his life—the experiences of his remarkable childhood, encounters with many saints and sages during his youthful search throughout India for an illumined teacher, ten years of training in the hermitage of a revered yoga master, and the thirty years that he lived and taught in America. Also recorded here are his meetings with Mahatma Gandhi, Rabindranath Tagore, Luther Burbank, the Catholic stigmatist Therese Neumann, and other celebrated spiritual personalities of East and West.

Autobiography of a Yogi is at once a beautifully written account of an exceptional life and a profound introduction to the ancient science of Yoga and its time-honored tradition of meditation. The author clearly explains the subtle but definite laws behind both the ordinary events of everyday life and the extraordinary events commonly termed miracles. His absorbing life story thus becomes the background for a penetrating and unforgettable look at the ultimate mysteries of human existence.

Considered a modern spiritual classic, the book has been translated into more than twenty-five languages and is widely used as a text and reference work in colleges and universities. A perennial best seller since it was first published more than sixty years ago, *Autobiography of a Yogi* has found its way into the hearts of millions of readers around the world.

"A rare account."—THE NEW YORK TIMES

"A fascinating and clearly annotated study."—NEWSWEEK

"There has been nothing before, written in English or in any other European language, like this presentation of Yoga."

—COLUMBIA UNIVERSITY PRESS

OTHER BOOKS BY PARAMAHANSA YOGANANDA

Available at bookstores or directly from the publisher:
Self-Realization Fellowship
3880 San Rafael Avenue • Los Angeles, California 90065
Tel (323) 225-2471 • Fax (323) 225-5088
www.yogananda-srf.org

God Talks With Arjuna: *The Bhagavad Gita—A New Translation and Commentary*

In this monumental two-volume work, Paramahansa Yogananda reveals the innermost essence of India's most renowned scripture. Exploring its psychological, spiritual, and metaphysical depths, he presents a sweeping chronicle of the soul's journey to enlightenment through the royal science of God-realization.

The Second Coming of Christ: *The Resurrection of the Christ Within You—A revelatory commentary on the original teachings of Jesus*

In this unprecedented masterwork of inspiration, almost 1700 pages in length, Paramahansa Yogananda takes the reader on a profoundly enriching journey through the four Gospels. Verse by verse, he illumines the universal path to oneness with God taught by Jesus to his immediate disciples but obscured through centuries of misinterpretation: "how to become like Christ, how to resurrect the Eternal Christ within one's self."

The Yoga of the Bhagavad Gita: *An Introduction to India's Universal Science of God-Realization*

A compilation of selections from Paramahansa Yogananda's in-depth, critically acclaimed translation of and commentary on the Bhagavad Gita, *God Talks With Arjuna,* this book presents truth-seekers with an ideal introduction to the Gita's timeless and universal teachings. Contains Yogananda's complete translation of the Bhagavad Gita, presented for the first time in uninterrupted sequential form.

Man's Eternal Quest

Paramahansa Yogananda's *Collected Talks and Essays* present in-depth discussions of the vast range of inspiring and universal truths that have captivated millions in his *Autobiography of a Yogi*. Volume I explores little-known and seldom-understood aspects of meditation, life after death, the nature of creation, health and healing, the unlimited powers of the mind, and the eternal quest that finds fulfillment only in God.

The Divine Romance
Volume II of Paramahansa Yogananda's collected talks and essays. Among the wide-ranging selections: *How to Cultivate Divine Love; Harmonizing Physical, Mental, and Spiritual Methods of Healing; A World Without Boundaries; Controlling Your Destiny; The Yoga Art of Overcoming Mortal Consciousness and Death; The Cosmic Lover; Finding the Joy in Life.*

Journey to Self-realization
Volume III of the collected talks and essays presents Sri Yogananda's unique combination of wisdom, compassion, down-to-earth guidance, and encouragement on dozens of fascinating subjects, including: *Quickening Human Evolution, How to Express Everlasting Youthfulness,* and *Realizing God in Your Daily Life.*

Wine of the Mystic: *The Rubaiyat of Omar Khayyam—A Spiritual Interpretation*
An inspired commentary that brings to light the mystical science of God-communion hidden behind the *Rubaiyat's* enigmatic imagery. Includes 50 original color illustrations. Winner of the 1995 Benjamin Franklin Award for best book in the field of religion.

Where There Is Light: *Insight and Inspiration for Meeting Life's Challenges*
Gems of thought arranged by subject; a unique handbook to which readers can quickly turn for a reassuring sense of direction in times of uncertainty or crisis, or for a renewed awareness of the ever present power of God one can draw upon in daily life.

Whispers from Eternity
A collection of Paramahansa Yogananda's prayers and divine experiences in the elevated states of meditation. Expressed in a majestic rhythm and poetic beauty, his words reveal the inexhaustible variety

of God's nature, and the infinite sweetness with which He responds to those who seek Him.

The Science of Religion
Within every human being, Paramahansa Yogananda writes, there is one inescapable desire: to overcome suffering and attain a happiness that does not end. Explaining how it is possible to fulfill these longings, he examines the relative effectiveness of the different approaches to this goal.

In the Sanctuary of the Soul: *A Guide to Effective Prayer*
Compiled from the works of Paramahansa Yogananda, this inspiring devotional companion reveals ways of making prayer a daily source of love, strength, and guidance.

Inner Peace: *How to Be Calmly Active and Actively Calm*
A practical and inspiring guide, compiled from the talks and writings of Paramahansa Yogananda, that demonstrates how we can be "actively calm" by creating peace through meditation, and "calmly active"—centered in the stillness and joy of our own essential nature while living a dynamic, fulfilling, and balanced life. Winner of the 2000 Benjamin Franklin Award—best book in the field of Metaphysics/Spirituality.

To Be Victorious in Life *(How-to-Live Series)*
In this powerful book, Paramahansa Yogananda shows how we can realize life's highest goals by bringing out the unlimited potential within us. He provides practical counsel for achieving success, outlines definite methods of creating lasting happiness, and tells how to overcome negativity and inertia by harnessing the dynamic power of our own will.

Living Fearlessly: *Bringing Out Your Inner Soul Strength (How-to-Live Series)*
Paramahansa Yogananda teaches us how to break the shackles of fear and reveals how we can overcome our own psychological stumbling blocks. *Living Fearlessly* is a testament to what we can become if we but have faith in the divinity of our true nature as the soul.

How You Can Talk With God
Defining God as both the transcendent, universal Spirit and the intimately personal Father, Mother, Friend, and Lover of all, Paramahansa Yogananda shows how close the Lord is to each one of us, and how He can be persuaded to "break His silence" and respond in a tangible way.

Metaphysical Meditations
More than 300 spiritually uplifting meditations, prayers, and affirmations that can be used to develop greater health and vitality, creativity, self-confidence, and calmness; and to live more fully in a conscious awareness of the blissful presence of God.

Scientific Healing Affirmations
Paramahansa Yogananda presents here a profound explanation of the science of affirmation. He makes clear why affirmations work, and how to use the power of word and thought not only to bring about healing but to effect desired change in every area of life. Includes a wide variety of affirmations.

Sayings of Paramahansa Yogananda
A collection of sayings and wise counsel that conveys Paramahansa Yogananda's candid and loving responses to those who came to him for guidance. Recorded by a number of his close disciples, the anecdotes in this book give the reader an opportunity to share in their personal encounters with the Master.

Songs of the Soul
Mystical poetry by Paramahansa Yogananda—an outpouring of his direct perceptions of God in the beauties of nature, in man, in everyday experiences, and in the spiritually awakened state of *samadhi* meditation.

The Law of Success
Explains dynamic principles for achieving one's goals in life, and outlines the universal laws that bring success and fulfillment—personal, professional, and spiritual.

Cosmic Chants: Spiritualized Songs for Divine Communion
Words and music to 60 songs of devotion, with an introduction explaining how spiritual chanting can lead to God-communion.

AUDIO RECORDINGS OF PARAMAHANSA YOGANANDA

- *Beholding the One in All*
- *Awake in the Cosmic Dream*
- *Songs of My Heart*
- *Be a Smile Millionaire*
- *The Great Light of God*
- *To Make Heaven on Earth*
- *One Life Versus Reincarnation*

- *Removing All Sorrow and Suffering*
- *In the Glory of the Spirit*
- *Follow the Path of Christ, Krishna, and the Masters*
- *Self-Realization: The Inner and the Outer Path*

OTHER PUBLICATIONS FROM SELF-REALIZATION FELLOWSHIP

The Holy Science by Swami Sri Yukteswar

Only Love: Living the Spiritual Life in a Changing World by Sri Daya Mata

Finding the Joy Within You: Personal Counsel for God-Centered Living by Sri Daya Mata

Enter the Quiet Heart: Creating a Loving Relationship With God by Sri Daya Mata

God Alone: The Life and Letters of a Saint by Sri Gyanamata

"Mejda": The Family and the Early Life of Paramahansa Yogananda by Sananda Lal Ghosh

Self-Realization (a quarterly magazine founded by Paramahansa Yogananda in 1925)

FREE INTRODUCTORY BOOKLET: *Undreamed-of Possibilities*

The scientific techniques of meditation taught by Paramahansa Yogananda, including *Kriya Yoga*—as well as his guidance on all aspects of balanced spiritual living—are taught in the *Self-Realization Fellowship Lessons*. For further information, please write for the free introductory booklet, *Undreamed-of Possibilities*.

A complete catalog describing all of the Self-Realization Fellowship publications and audio/video recordings is available on request.

Aims and Ideals
of
Self-Realization Fellowship

As set forth by Paramahansa Yogananda, Founder
Sri Mrinalini Mata, President

To disseminate among the nations a knowledge of definite scientific techniques for attaining direct personal experience of God.

To teach that the purpose of life is the evolution, through self-effort, of man's limited mortal consciousness into God Consciousness; and to this end to establish Self-Realization Fellowship temples for God-communion throughout the world, and to encourage the establishment of individual temples of God in the homes and in the hearts of men.

To reveal the complete harmony and basic oneness of original Christianity as taught by Jesus Christ and original Yoga as taught by Bhagavan Krishna; and to show that these principles of truth are the common scientific foundation of all true religions.

To point out the one divine highway to which all paths of true religious beliefs eventually lead; the highway of daily, scientific, devotional meditation on God.

To liberate man from his threefold suffering: physical disease, mental inharmonies, and spiritual ignorance.

To encourage "plain living and high thinking"; and to spread a spirit of brotherhood among all peoples by teaching the eternal basis of their unity: kinship with God.

To demonstrate the superiority of mind over body, of soul over mind.

To overcome evil by good, sorrow by joy, cruelty by kindness, ignorance by wisdom.

To unite science and religion through realization of the unity of their underlying principles.

To advocate cultural and spiritual understanding between East and West, and the exchange of their finest distinctive features.

To serve mankind as one's larger Self.

GLOSSARY

Arjuna. The exalted disciple to whom Bhagavan Krishna imparted the immortal message of the Bhagavad Gita *(q.v.)*; one of the five Pandava princes in the great Hindu epic, the *Mahabharata,* in which he is a key figure.

astral body. Man's subtle body of light, *prana* or lifetrons; the second of three sheaths that successively encase the soul: the causal body *(q.v.),* the astral body, and the physical body. The powers of the astral body enliven the physical body, much as electricity illumines a bulb. The astral body has nineteen elements: intelligence, ego, feeling, mind (sense-consciousness); five instruments of knowledge (the sensory powers within the physical organs of sight, hearing, smell, taste, and touch); five instruments of action (the executive powers in the physical instruments of procreation, excretion, speech, locomotion, and the exercise of manual skill); and five instruments of life force that perform the functions of circulation, metabolization, assimilation, crystallization, and elimination.

astral world. The subtle sphere of the Lord's creation, a universe of light and color composed of finer-than-atomic forces, i.e., vibrations of life energy or lifetrons (see *prana*). Every being, every object, every vibration on the material plane has an astral counterpart, for in the astral universe (heaven) is the blueprint of our material universe. At physical death, the soul of man, clothed in an astral body of light, ascends to one of the higher or lower astral planes, according to merit, to continue his spiritual evolution in the greater freedom of that subtle realm. There he remains for a karmically predetermined time until physical rebirth.

Aum (Om). The Sanskrit root word or seed-sound symbolizing that aspect of Godhead which creates and sustains all things; Cosmic Vibration. *Aum* of the Vedas became the sacred word *Hum* of the Tibetans; *Amin* of the Moslems; and *Amen* of the Egyptians, Greeks, Romans, Jews, and Christians. The world's great religions state that all created things originate in the cosmic vibratory energy of *Aum* or Amen, the Word or Holy Ghost. "In the beginning was the Word, and the Word was with God, and the Word was God....All things were made by him [the Word or *Aum*]; and without him was not any thing made that was made" (John 1:1, 3).

Amen in Hebrew means *sure, faithful.* "These things saith the Amen, the faithful and true witness, the beginning of the creation of God" (Revelation 3:14). Even as sound is produced by the vibration of a running motor, so the omnipresent sound of *Aum* faithfully testifies to the running of the "Cosmic Motor," which upholds all life and every particle of creation through vibratory energy. In the *Self-Realization Fellowship Lessons (q.v.),* Paramahansa Yogananda teaches techniques of meditation whose practice brings direct experience of God as *Aum* or Holy Ghost. That blissful communion with the invisible divine Power ("the Comforter, which is the Holy Ghost"—John 14:26) is the truly scientific basis of prayer.

avatar. From the Sanskrit *avatara*, with roots *ava*, "down," and *tri*, "to pass." Souls who attain union with Spirit and then return to earth to help mankind are called avatars, divine incarnations.

avidya. Literally, "non-knowledge," ignorance; the manifestation in man of *maya*, the cosmic delusion *(q.v.)*. Essentially, *avidya* is man's ignorance of his divine nature and of the sole reality: Spirit.

Babaji. See *Mahavatar Babaji*.

Bhagavad Gita. "Song of the Lord." An ancient Indian scripture consisting of eighteen chapters from the sixth book (*Bhishma Parva*) of the *Mahabharata* epic. Presented in the form of a dialogue between the avatar *(q.v.)* Lord Krishna and his disciple Arjuna on the eve of the historic battle of Kurukshetra, the Gita is a profound treatise on the science of Yoga (union with God) and a timeless prescription for happiness and success in everyday living. The Gita is allegory as well as history, a spiritual dissertation on the inner battle between man's good and bad tendencies. Depending on the context, Krishna symbolizes the guru, the soul, or God; Arjuna represents the aspiring devotee. Of this universal scripture Mahatma Gandhi wrote: "Those who will meditate on the Gita will derive fresh joy and new meanings from it every day. There is not a single spiritual tangle which the Gita cannot unravel."

The quotations from the Bhagavad Gita in this book are from Paramahansa Yogananda's own translation, *God Talks With Arjuna: The Bhagavad Gita—Royal Science of God-Realization* (published by Self-Realization Fellowship).

Bhagavan Krishna. An avatar who lived as a king in India ages before the Christian era. One of the meanings given for the word *Krishna* in the Hindu scriptures is "Omniscient Spirit." Thus, *Krishna*, like *Christ*, is a spiritual title signifying the divine magnitude of the avatar—his oneness with God. The title *Bhagavan* means "Lord." In his early life, Krishna lived as a cowherd who enchanted his companions with the music of his flute. In this role Krishna is often considered to represent allegorically the soul playing the flute of meditation to guide all misled thoughts back to the fold of omniscience.

Bhakti Yoga. The spiritual approach to God that stresses all-surrendering love as the principal means for communion and union with God. See *Yoga*.

Brahman (Brahma). Absolute Spirit. Brahman is sometimes rendered in Sanskrit as *Brahma* (with a short *a* at the end); but the meaning is the same as Brahman: Spirit, or God the Father, not the circumscribed concept of the personal "Brahma-the-Creator" of the Brahma-Vishnu-Shiva triad (which is rendered with a long *ā* at the end, *Brahmā*).

breath. "The influx of innumerable cosmic currents into man by way of the breath induces restlessness in his mind," Paramahansa Yogananda wrote. "Thus the breath links him with the fleeting phenomenal worlds. To escape from the sorrows of transitoriness and to enter the blissful realm of Reality, the yogi learns to quiet the breath by scientific meditation."

causal body. Essentially, man as a soul is a causal-bodied being. His causal body is an idea-matrix for the astral and physical bodies. The causal body is composed of 35 idea elements corresponding to the 19 elements of the astral body *(q.v.)* plus the 16 basic material elements of the physical body.

causal world. Behind the physical world of matter (atoms, protons, electrons), and the subtle astral world of luminous life energy (lifetrons), is the causal, or ideational, world of thought (thoughtrons). After man evolves sufficiently to transcend the physical and astral universes, he resides in the causal universe. In the consciousness of causal beings, the physical and astral universes are resolved to their thought essence. Whatever physical man can do in imagination, causal man can do in actuality—the only limitation being thought itself. Ultimately, man sheds the last soul covering—his causal body—to unite with omnipresent Spirit, beyond all vibratory realms.

chakras. In Yoga, the seven occult centers of life and consciousness in the spine and brain, which enliven the physical and astral bodies of man. These centers are referred to as *chakras* ("wheels") because the concentrated energy in each one is like a hub from which radiate rays of life-giving light and energy. In ascending order, these *chakras* are *muladhara* (the coccygeal, at the base of the spine); *svadhisthana* (the sacral, two inches above *muladhara*); *manipura* (the lumbar, opposite the navel); *anahata* (the dorsal, opposite the heart); *vishuddha* (the cervical, at the base of the neck); *ajna* (traditionally located between the eyebrows; in actuality, directly connected by polarity with the medulla; see also *medulla* and *spiritual eye*); and *sahasrara* (in the uppermost part of the cerebrum).

The seven centers are divinely planned exits or "trap doors" through which the soul has descended into the body and through which it must reascend by a process of meditation. By seven successive steps, the soul escapes into Cosmic Consciousness. In its conscious upward passage through the seven opened or "awakened" cerebrospinal centers, the soul travels the highway to the Infinite, the true path by which the soul must retrace its course to reunite with God.

Yoga treatises generally consider only the six lower centers as *chakras,* with *sahasrara* referred to separately as a seventh center. All seven centers, however, are often referred to as lotuses, whose petals open, or turn upward, in spiritual awakening as the life and consciousness travel up the spine.

chitta. Intuitive feeling; the aggregate of consciousness, inherent in which is *ahamkara* (egoity), *buddhi* (intelligence), and *manas* (mind or sense consciousness).

Christ. The honorific title of Jesus: Jesus the Christ. This term also denotes God's universal intelligence immanent in creation (sometimes referred to as the Cosmic Christ or the Infinite Christ), or is used in reference to great masters who have attained oneness with that Divine Consciousness. (The Greek word *Christos* means "anointed," as does the Hebrew word *Messiah.)* See also *Christ Consciousness* and *Kutastha Chaitanya.*

Christ center. The *Kutastha* or *ajna chakra* at the point between the eyebrows, directly connected by polarity with the medulla *(q.v.);* center of will and concentration, and of Christ Consciousness *(q.v.);* seat of the spiritual eye *(q.v.).*

Christ Consciousness. The projected consciousness of God immanent in all creation. In Christian scripture, the "only begotten son," the only pure reflection in creation of God the Father; in Hindu scripture, *Kutastha Chaitanya* or *Tat,* the universal consciousness, or cosmic intelligence, of Spirit everywhere present in creation. (The terms "Christ Consciousness" and "Christ Intelligence" are synonymous, as also "Cosmic Christ" and "Infinite Christ.") It is the universal consciousness, oneness with God, manifested by Jesus, Krishna, and other avatars. Great saints and yogis know it as the state of *samadhi* meditation wherein their consciousness has become identified with the divine intelligence in every particle of creation; they feel the entire universe as their own body. See *Trinity.*

consciousness, states of. In mortal consciousness man experiences three states: waking consciousness, sleeping consciousness, and dreaming consciousness. But he does not experience his soul, superconsciousness, and he does not experience God. The Christ-man does. As mortal man is conscious throughout his body, so the Christ-man is conscious throughout the universe, which he feels as his body. Beyond the state of Christ consciousness is cosmic consciousness, the experience of oneness with God in His absolute consciousness beyond vibratory creation as well as with the Lord's omnipresence manifesting in the phenomenal worlds.

Cosmic Consciousness. The Absolute; transcendental Spirit existing beyond creation; God the Father. Also the *samadhi*-meditation state of oneness with God both beyond and within vibratory creation. See *Trinity.*

cosmic delusion. See *maya.*

cosmic energy. See *prana.*

Cosmic Intelligent Vibration. See *Aum.*

Cosmic Sound. See *Aum.*

dharma. Eternal principles of righteousness that uphold all creation; man's inherent duty to live in harmony with these principles. See also *Sanatana Dharma.*

disciple. A spiritual aspirant who comes to a guru seeking introduction to God, and to this end establishes an eternal spiritual relationship with the guru. In Self-Realization Fellowship, the guru-disciple relationship is established by *diksha,* initiation, in *Kriya Yoga.* See also *guru* and *Kriya Yoga.*

Divine Mother. The aspect of God that is active in creation; the *shakti,* or power, of the Transcendent Creator. Other terms for this aspect of Divinity are *Aum, Shakti,* Holy Ghost, Cosmic Intelligent Vibration, Nature or *Prakriti.* Also, the personal aspect of God embodying the love and compassionate qualities of a mother.

The Hindu scriptures teach that God is both immanent and transcendent, personal and impersonal. He may be sought as the Absolute; as one of His manifest eternal qualities, such as love, wisdom, bliss, light; in the form of an *ishta* (deity); or as Father, Mother, or Friend.

egoism. The ego-principle, *ahamkara* (lit., "I do"), is the root cause of dualism or the seeming separation between man and his Creator. *Ahamkara* brings human beings under the sway of *maya (q.v.)*, by which the subject (ego) falsely appears as object; the creatures imagine themselves to be creators. By banishing ego-consciousness, man awakens to his divine identity, his oneness with the Sole Life: God.

elements (five). The Cosmic Vibration, or *Aum*, structures all physical creation, including man's physical body, through the manifestation of five *tattvas* (elements): earth, water, fire, air, and ether *(q.v.)*. These are structural forces, intelligent and vibratory in nature. Without the earth element there would be no state of solid matter; without the water element, no liquid state; without the air element, no gaseous state; without the fire element, no heat; without the ether element, no background on which to produce the cosmic motion picture show. In the body, *prana* (cosmic vibratory energy) enters the medulla and is then divided into the five elemental currents by the action of the five lower *chakras (q.v.)*, or centers: the coccygeal (earth), sacral (water), lumbar (fire), dorsal (air), and cervical (ether). The Sanskrit terminology for these elements is *prithivi, ap, tej, prana,* and *akasha.*

ether. The Sanskrit word *akaśa*, translated as both "ether" and "space," refers specifically to the vibratory element that is the subtlest in the material world. (See *elements.*) It derives from *ā*, "towards" and *kasha*, "to be visible, to appear." *Akasha* is the subtle "background" against which everything in the material universe becomes perceptible. "Space gives dimension to objects; ether separates the images," Paramahansa Yogananda said. "Ether-permeated space is the boundary line between heaven, or the astral world, and earth," he explained. "All the finer forces God has created are composed of light, or thought-forms, and are merely hidden behind a particular vibration that manifests as ether."

evil. The satanic force that obscures God's omnipresence in creation, manifesting as inharmonies in man and nature. Also, a broad term defining anything contrary to divine law (see *dharma*) that causes man to lose the consciousness of his essential unity with God, and that obstructs attainment of God-realization.

guru. Spiritual teacher. Though the word *guru* is often misused to refer simply to any teacher or instructor, a true God-illumined guru is one who, in his attainment of self-mastery, has realized his identity with the omnipresent Spirit. Such a one is uniquely qualified to lead the seeker on his or her inward journey toward divine realization.

When a devotee is ready to seek God in earnest, the Lord sends him a guru. Through the wisdom, intelligence, Self-realization, and teachings of such a master, God guides the disciple. By following the master's teachings and discipline, the disciple is able to fulfill his soul's desire for the manna of God-perception. A true guru, ordained by God to help sincere seekers in response to their deep soul craving, is not an ordinary teacher: he is a human vehicle whose body, speech, mind, and spirituality God uses as a channel to attract and guide lost souls back to their home of immortality. A guru is a living embodiment of scriptural truth. He is an agent of salvation appointed by God in response to a devotee's demand for release from the bondage of matter.

"To keep company with the Guru," wrote Swami Sri Yukteswar in *The Holy Science*, "is not only to be in his physical presence (as this is sometimes impossible), but mainly means to keep him in our hearts and to be one with him in principle and to attune ourselves with him." See *master*.

Gurus of Self-Realization Fellowship. The Gurus of Self-Realization Fellowship (Yogoda Satsanga Society of India) are Jesus Christ, Bhagavan Krishna, and a line of exalted masters of contemporary times: Mahavatar Babaji, Lahiri Mahasaya, Swami Sri Yukteswar, and Paramahansa Yogananda. To show the harmony and essential unity of the teachings of Jesus Christ and the Yoga precepts of Bhagavan Krishna is an integral part of the SRF dispensation. All of these Gurus, by their universal teachings and divine instrumentality, contribute to the fulfillment of the Self-Realization Fellowship mission of bringing to humanity a practical spiritual science of God-realization.

The passing of a guru's spiritual mantle to a disciple designated to carry on the lineage to which that guru belongs is termed *guru parampara*. Thus Paramahansa Yogananda's direct lineage of gurus is Mahavatar Babaji, Lahiri Mahasaya, and Swami Sri Yukteswar.

Before his passing Paramahansaji stated that it was God's wish that he be the last in the Self-Realization Fellowship line of Gurus. No succeeding disciple or leader in his society will ever assume the title of guru. "When I am gone," he said, "the teachings will be the guru....Through the teachings you will be in tune with me and the great Gurus who sent me."

When questioned about the succession of the presidency of Self-Realization Fellowship/Yogoda Satsanga Society of India, Paramahansaji stated: "There will always be at the head of this organization men and women of realization. They are already known to God and the Gurus. They shall serve as my spiritual successor and representative in all spiritual and organizational matters."

Holy Ghost. The sacred Cosmic Intelligent Vibration projected from God to structure and sustain creation from Its own vibratory Essence. It is thus the Holy Presence of God, His Word, omnipresent in the universe and in every form, vehicle of God's perfect universal reflection, Christ Consciousness *(q.v.)*. The Comforter, Cosmic Mother Nature, Prakriti *(q.v.)*. See *Aum* and *Trinity*.

"Holy Ghost" is synonymous with "Holy Spirit"—the term used in many modern English versions of the Bible. Both are translations of the same Greek and Hebrew words. *Ruach* in Hebrew and *pneuma* in Greek are used to signify a range of concepts: spirit, breath, and wind—in general, the life principle of man and the cosmos. (Similarly in Latin, in which *inspiration* refers to the inflow of breath as well as of divine or creative spirit; and in Sanskrit, in which *prana* denotes the breath as well as the subtle astral life energy that sustains the body, and the universal Cosmic Vibratory Energy that underlies and upholds every particle of creation.) At the time of the King James translation of the Bible, both "spirit" and "ghost" in English conveyed the same meaning as *ruach* and *pneuma;* the everyday connotation of "ghost" has changed in the centuries since then. The King James rendering, used in this book, avoids confusion between Spirit (the transcendental God the Father) and Its activating Creative Vibratory Energy (Holy Ghost).

intuition. The all-knowing faculty of the soul, which enables man to experience direct perception of truth without the intermediary of the senses.

Jnana Yoga. (Pronounced *gyana yoga.*) The path to union with God through transmutation of the discriminative power of the intellect into the omniscient wisdom of the soul.

karma. Effects of past actions, from this or previous lifetimes; from the Sanskrit *kri,* to do. The equilibrating law of karma, as expounded in the Hindu scriptures, is that of action and reaction, cause and effect, sowing and reaping. In the course of natural righteousness, each man by his thoughts and actions becomes the molder of his destiny. Whatever energies he himself, wisely or unwisely, has set in motion must return to him as their starting point, like a circle inexorably completing itself. An understanding of karma as the law of justice serves to free the human mind from resentment against God and man. A man's karma follows him from incarnation to incarnation until fulfilled or spiritually transcended. See *reincarnation.*

The cumulative actions of human beings within communities, nations, or the world as a whole constitute mass karma, which produces local or far-ranging effects according to the degree and preponderance of good or evil. The thoughts and actions of every man, therefore, contribute to the good or ill of this world and all peoples in it.

Karma Yoga. The path to God through nonattached action and service. By selfless service, by giving the fruits of one's actions to God, and by seeing God as the sole Doer, the devotee becomes free of the ego and experiences God. See *Yoga.*

Krishna. See *Bhagavan Krishna.*

Krishna Consciousness. Christ Consciousness; *Kutastha Chaitanya.* See *Christ Consciousness.*

Kriya Yoga. A sacred spiritual science, originating millenniums ago in India. It includes certain techniques of meditation whose devoted practice leads to realization of God. Paramahansa Yogananda has explained that the Sanskrit root of *kriya* is *kri,* to do, to act and react; the same root is found in the word *karma,* the natural principle of cause and effect. Kriya Yoga is thus "union (*yoga*) with the Infinite through a certain action or rite (*kriya*)." Kriya Yoga is praised by Krishna in the Bhagavad Gita and by Patanjali in the *Yoga Sutras.* Revived in this age by Mahavatar Babaji *(q.v.),* Kriya Yoga is the *diksha* (spiritual initiation) bestowed by the Gurus of Self-Realization Fellowship. Since the *mahasamadhi (q.v.)* of Paramahansa Yogananda, *diksha* is conferred through his appointed spiritual representative, the president of Self-Realization Fellowship/Yogoda Satsanga Society of India (or through one appointed by the president). To qualify for *diksha* Self-Realization members must fulfill certain preliminary spiritual requirements. One who has received this *diksha* is a *Kriya Yogi* or *Kriyaban.* See also *guru* and *disciple.*

kundalini. The powerful current of creative life energy residing in a subtle coiled passageway at the base of the spine. In ordinary waking consciousness, the body's life force flows from the brain down the spine and out through this coiled *kundalini* passage, enlivening the physical body and tying the astral and causal bodies *(qq.v.)* and the indwelling soul to the mortal form. In the higher states of consciousness that are the goal of meditation, the *kundalini* energy is reversed to flow back up the spine to awaken the dormant spiritual faculties in the cerebrospinal centers (*chakras*). Also called the "serpent force," because of its coiled configuration.

Kutastha Chaitanya. Christ Consciousness *(q.v.).* The Sanskrit word *kutastha* means "that which remains unchanged"; *chaitanya* means consciousness.

Lahiri Mahasaya. *Lahiri* was the family name of Shyama Charan Lahiri (1828–1895). *Mahasaya,* a Sanskrit religious title, means "large-minded." Lahiri Mahasaya was a disciple of Mahavatar Babaji, and the guru of Swami Sri Yukteswar (Paramahansa Yogananda's guru). Lahiri Mahasaya was the one to whom Babaji revealed the ancient, almost-lost science of *Kriya Yoga (q.v.).* A *Yogavatar* ("Incarnation of Yoga"), he was a seminal figure in the renaissance of yoga in modern India who gave instruction and blessing to countless seekers who came to him, without regard to caste or creed. He was a Christlike teacher with miraculous powers; but also a family man with business responsibilities, who demonstrated for the modern world how an ideally balanced life can be achieved by combining meditation with right performance of outer duties. Lahiri Mahasaya's life is described in *Autobiography of a Yogi.*

life force. See *prana.*

lifetrons. See *prana.*

Mahavatar Babaji. The deathless *Mahavatar* ("great avatar") who in 1861 gave *Kriya Yoga (q.v.)* initiation to Lahiri Mahasaya, and thereby restored to the world the ancient technique of salvation. Perennially youthful, he has lived for centuries in the Himalayas, bestowing a constant blessing on the world. His mission has been to assist prophets in carrying out their special dispensations. Many titles signifying his exalted spiritual stature have been given to him, but the *mahavatar* has generally adopted the simple name of Babaji, from the Sanskrit *baba*, "father," and the suffix *ji*, denoting respect. More information about his life and spiritual mission is given in *Autobiography of a Yogi.* See *avatar.*

man. The word is derived from the same root as Sanskrit *manas,* mind—the uniquely human capacity for rational thought. The science of yoga deals with human consciousness from the point of view of the essentially androgynous Self (*atman*). As there is no other terminology in English that would convey these psychological and spiritual truths without excessive literary awkwardness, the use of *man* and related terms has been retained in this publication — not in the narrowly exclusive sense of the word *man*, denoting only half of the human race, but in its broader original meaning.

Mantra Yoga. Divine communion attained through devotional, concentrated repetition of root-word sounds that have a spiritually beneficial vibratory potency. See *Yoga*.

master. One who has achieved self-mastery. Also, a respectful term of address for one's guru (*q.v.*).

Paramahansa Yogananda has pointed out that "the distinguishing qualifications of a master are not physical but spiritual....Proof that one is a master is supplied only by the ability to enter at will the breathless state (*savikalpa samadhi*) and by the attainment of immutable bliss (*nirvikalpa samadhi*)." See *samadhi*.

Paramahansaji further states: "All scriptures proclaim that the Lord created man in His omnipotent image. Control over the universe appears to be supernatural, but in truth such power is inherent and natural in everyone who attains 'right remembrance' of his divine origin. Men of God-realization...are devoid of the ego-principle (*ahamkara*) and its uprisings of personal desires; the actions of true masters are in effortless conformity with *rita*, natural righteousness. In Emerson's words, 'all great ones become "not virtuous, but Virtue; then is the end of the creation answered, and God is well pleased." '"

maya. The delusory power inherent in the structure of creation, by which the One appears as many. *Maya* is the principle of relativity, inversion, contrast, duality, oppositional states; the "Satan" (lit., in Hebrew, "the adversary") of the Old Testament prophets; and the "devil" whom Christ described picturesquely as a "murderer" and a "liar," because "there is no truth in him" (John 8:44).

Paramahansa Yogananda wrote:"The Sanskrit word *maya* means 'the measurer'; it is the magical power in creation by which limitations and divisions are apparently present in the Immeasurable and Inseparable. *Maya* is Nature herself — the phenomenal worlds, ever in transitional flux as antithesis to Divine Immutability.

"In God's plan and play (*lila*), the sole function of Satan or *maya* is to attempt to divert man from Spirit to matter, from Reality to unreality. 'The devil sinneth from the beginning. For this purpose the Son of God was manifested, that he might destroy the works of the devil' (I John 3:8). That is, the manifestation of Christ Consciousness, within man's own being, effortlessly destroys the illusions or 'works of the devil.'

"*Maya* is the veil of transitoriness in Nature, the ceaseless becoming of creation; the veil that each man must lift in order to see behind it the Creator, the changeless Immutable, eternal Reality."

meditation. Generally, interiorized concentration with the objective of perceiving God. True meditation, *dhyana,* is conscious realization of God through intuitive perception. It is achieved only after the devotee has attained that fixed concentration whereby he disconnects his attention from the senses and is completely undisturbed by sensory impressions from the outer world. *Dhyana* is the seventh step of Patanjali's Eightfold Path of Yoga, the eighth step being *samadhi,* communion, oneness with God. See *Patanjali.*

medulla oblongata. This structure at the base of the brain (top of the spinal cord) is the principal point of entry of life force *(prana)* into the body. It is the seat of the sixth cerebrospinal center, whose function is to receive and direct the incoming flow of cosmic energy. The life force is stored in the seventh center *(sahasrara)* in the topmost part of the brain. From that reservoir it is distributed throughout the body. The subtle center at the medulla is the main switch that controls the entrance, storage, and distribution of the life force.

paramahansa. A spiritual title signifying a master *(q.v.).* It may be conferred only by a true guru on a qualified disciple. Paramahansa literally means "supreme swan." In the Hindu scriptures, the *hansa* or swan symbolizes spiritual discrimination. Swami Sri Yukteswar bestowed the title on his beloved disciple Yogananda in 1935.

Patanjali. Renowned exponent of yoga, a sage of ancient times, whose *Yoga Sutras* outline the principles of the yogic path, dividing it into eight steps: (1) moral proscriptions *(yama),* (2) right observances *(niyama),* (3) meditation posture *(asana),* (4) life-force control *(pranayama),* (5) interiorization of the mind *(pratyahara),* (6) concentration *(dharana),* (7) meditation *(dhyana),* (8) union with God *(samadhi).*

prana. Sparks of intelligent finer-than-atomic energy that constitute life, collectively referred to in Hindu scriptural treatises as *prana,* which Paramahansa Yogananda has translated as "lifetrons." In essence, condensed thoughts of God; substance of the astral world *(q.v.)* and life principle of the physical cosmos. In the physical world, there are two kinds of *prana:* (1) the cosmic vibratory energy that is omnipresent in the universe, structuring and sustaining all things; (2) the specific *prana* or energy that pervades and sustains each human body through five currents or functions. *Prana* current performs the function of crystallization; *vyana* current, circulation; *samana* current, assimilation; *udana* current, metabolism; and *apana* current, elimination.

pranayama. Conscious control of *prana* (the creative vibration or energy that activates and sustains life in the body). The yoga science of *pranayama* is the direct way to consciously disconnect the mind from the life functions and sensory perceptions that tie man to body-consciousness. *Pranayama* thus frees man's consciousness to commune with God. All scientific techniques that bring about union of soul and Spirit may be classified as yoga, and *pranayama* is the greatest yogic method for attaining this divine union.

Raja Yoga. The "royal" or highest path to God-union. It teaches scientific meditation *(q.v.)* as the ultimate means for realizing God, and includes the highest essentials from all other forms of yoga. The Self-Realization Fellowship *Raja Yoga* teachings outline a way of life leading to perfect unfoldment in body, mind, and soul, based on the foundation of *Kriya Yoga (q.v.)* meditation. See *yoga*.

reincarnation. The doctrine that human beings, compelled by the law of evolution, incarnate repeatedly in progressively higher lives—retarded by wrong actions and desires, and advanced by spiritual endeavors—until Self-realization and God-union are attained. Having thus transcended the limitations and imperfections of mortal consciousness, the soul is forever freed from compulsory reincarnation. "Him that overcometh will I make a pillar in the temple of my God, and he shall go no more out" (Revelation 3:12).

rishis. Seers, exalted beings who manifest divine wisdom; especially, the illumined sages of ancient India to whom the Vedas were intuitively revealed.

sadhana. Path of spiritual discipline. The specific instruction and meditation practices prescribed by the guru for his disciples, who by faithfully following them ultimately realize God.

samadhi. The highest step on the Eightfold Path of Yoga, as outlined by the sage Patanjali *(q.v.)*. *Samadhi* is attained when the meditator, the process of meditation (by which the mind is withdrawn from the senses by interiorization), and the object of meditation (God) become One. Paramahansa Yogananda has explained that "in the initial states of God-communion (*savikalpa samadhi*) the devotee's consciousness merges in the Cosmic Spirit; his life force is withdrawn from the body, which appears 'dead,' or motionless and rigid. The yogi is fully aware of his bodily condition of suspended animation. As he progresses to higher spiritual states (*nirvikalpa samadhi*), however, he communes with God without bodily fixation; and in his ordinary waking consciousness, even in the midst of exacting worldly duties." Both states are characterized by oneness with the ever new bliss of Spirit, but the *nirvikalpa* state is experienced by only the most highly advanced masters.

Sanatana Dharma. Literally, "eternal religion." The name given to the body of Vedic teachings that came to be called Hinduism after the Greeks designated the people on the banks of the river Indus as *Indoos*, or *Hindus*. See *dharma*.

Satan. Literally, in Hebrew, "the adversary." Satan is the conscious and independent universal force that keeps everything and everybody deluded with the unspiritual consciousness of finiteness and separateness from God. To accomplish this, Satan uses the weapons of *maya* (cosmic delusion) and *avidya* (individual delusion, ignorance). See *maya*.

Self. Capitalized to denote the *atman* or soul, as distinguished from the ordinary self, which is the personality or ego *(q.v.)*. The Self is individualized Spirit, whose nature is ever-existing, ever-conscious, ever-new joy. Experience of these divine qualities of the soul's nature is achieved through meditation.

Self-realization. Paramahansa Yogananda has defined Self-realization as "the knowing—in body, mind, and soul—that we are one with the omnipresence of God; that we do not have to pray that it come to us, that we are not merely near it at all times, but that God's omnipresence is our omnipresence; that we are just as much a part of Him now as we ever will be. All we have to do is improve our knowing."

Self-Realization Fellowship. The international nonsectarian religious society founded by Paramahansa Yogananda in the United States in 1920 (and as Yogoda Satsanga Society of India in 1917) to disseminate worldwide the spiritual principles and meditation techniques of *Kriya Yoga,* and to foster greater understanding among people of all races, cultures, and creeds of the one Truth underlying all religions. (See "Aims and Ideals of Self-Realization Fellowship," page 126.)

Paramahansa Yogananda has explained that the name Self-Realization Fellowship signifies "fellowship with God through Self-realization, and friendship with all truth-seeking souls."

From its international headquarters in Los Angeles, the society publishes Paramahansa Yogananda's writings, lectures, and informal talks—including his comprehensive series of *Self-Realization Fellowship Lessons* for home study and *Self-Realization,* the magazine he founded in 1925; produces audio and video recordings on his teachings; oversees its temples, retreats, meditation centers, youth programs, and the monastic communities of the Self-Realization Order; conducts lecture and class series in cities around the world; and coordinates the Worldwide Prayer Circle, a network of groups and individuals dedicated to praying for those in need of physical, mental, or spiritual aid and for global peace and harmony.

Self-Realization Fellowship Lessons. The teachings of Paramahansa Yogananda, sent to students throughout the world in a series of lessons, available to all earnest truth-seekers. These lessons contain the yoga meditation techniques taught by Paramahansa Yogananda, including, for those who qualify, *Kriya Yoga (q.v.).*

soul. Individualized Spirit. The soul is the true and immortal nature of man, and of all living forms of life; it is cloaked only temporarily in the garments of causal, astral, and physical bodies. The nature of the soul is Spirit: ever-existing, ever-conscious, ever-new Joy.

spiritual eye. The single eye of intuition and omnipresent perception at the Christ (*Kutastha*) center (*ajna chakra*) between the eyebrows. The deeply meditating devotee beholds the spiritual eye as a ring of golden light encircling a sphere of opalescent blue, and at the center, a pentagonal white star. Microcosmically, these forms and colors epitomize, respectively, the vibratory realm of creation (Cosmic Nature, Holy Ghost); the Son or intelligence of God in creation (Christ

Consciousness); and the vibrationless Spirit beyond all creation (God the Father).

The spiritual eye is the entryway into the ultimate states of divine consciousness. In deep meditation, as the devotee's consciousness penetrates the spiritual eye, into the three realms epitomized therein, he experiences successively the following states: superconsciousness or the ever new joy of soul-realization, and oneness with God as *Aum (q.v.)* or Holy Ghost; Christ consciousness, oneness with the universal intelligence of God in all creation; and cosmic consciousness, unity with the omnipresence of God that is beyond as well as within vibratory manifestation. See also *consciousness, states of; superconsciousness; Christ Consciouness.*

Explaining a passage from Ezekiel (43:1–2), Paramahansa Yogananda has written: "Through the divine eye in the forehead, ('the east'), the yogi sails his consciousness into omnipresence, hearing the word or *Aum,* the divine sound of 'many waters': the vibrations of light that constitute the sole reality of creation." In Ezekiel's words: "Afterwards he brought me to the gate, even the gate that looketh towards the east; and behold, the glory of the God of Israel came from the way of the east; and his voice was like the noise of many waters; and the earth shined with his glory."

Jesus also spoke of the spiritual eye: "When thine eye is single, thy whole body also is full of light....Take heed therefore that the light which is in thee be not darkness" (Luke 11:34–35).

Sri. A title of respect. When used before the name of a religious person, it means "holy" or "revered."

Sri Yukteswar, Swami. Swami Sri Yukteswar Giri (1855–1936), India's Jnanavatar, "Incarnation of Wisdom"; guru of Paramahansa Yogananda, and *paramguru* of Self-Realization Fellowship *Kriyaban* members. Sri Yukteswarji was a disciple of Lahiri Mahasaya. At the behest of Lahiri Mahasaya's guru, Mahavatar Babaji, he wrote *The Holy Science,* a treatise on the underlying unity of Christian and Hindu scriptures, and trained Paramahansa Yogananda for his spiritual world-mission: the dissemination of *Kriya Yoga (q.v.).* Paramahansaji has lovingly described Sri Yukteswarji's life in *Autobiography of a Yogi.*

superconscious mind. The all-knowing power of the soul that perceives truth directly; intuition.

superconsciousness. The pure, intuitive, all-seeing, ever-blissful consciousness of the soul. Sometimes used generally to refer to all the various states of *samadhi (q.v.)* experienced in meditation, but specifically the first state of *samadhi,* wherein one drops ego-consciousness and realizes his self as soul, made in the image of God. Thence follow the higher states of realization: Christ consciousness and cosmic consciousness *(q.v.).*

Trinity. When Spirit manifests creation, It becomes the Trinity: Father, Son, Holy Ghost, or *Sat, Tat, Aum.* The Father (*Sat*) is God as the Creator existing beyond creation (Cosmic Consciousness). The Son (*Tat*) is God's omnipresent intelligence existing in creation (Christ Consciousness or *Kutastha Chaitanya*). The Holy Ghost (*Aum*) is the vibratory power of God that objectifies and becomes creation.

Vedas. The four scriptural texts of the Hindus: Rig Veda, Sama Veda, Yajur Veda, and Atharva Veda. They are essentially a literature of chant, ritual, and recitation for vitalizing and spiritualizing all phases of man's life and activity. Among the immense texts of India, the Vedas (Sanskrit root *vid*, "to know") are the only writings to which no author is ascribed. The Rig Veda assigns a celestial origin to the hymns and tells us they have come down from "ancient times," reclothed in new language. Divinely revealed from age to age to the *rishis*, "seers," the four Vedas are said to possess *nityatva*, "timeless finality."

Yoga. From Sanskrit *yuj*, "union." The highest connotation of the word *yoga* in Hindu philosophy is union of the individual soul with Spirit through scientific methods of meditation. Within the larger spectrum of Hindu philosophy, Yoga is one of six orthodox systems: *Vedanta, Mimamsa, Sankhya, Vaisesika, Nyaya,* and *Yoga.* There are also various types of yoga methods: *Hatha Yoga, Mantra Yoga, Laya Yoga, Karma Yoga, Jnana Yoga, Bhakti Yoga,* and *Raja Yoga. Raja Yoga,* the "royal" or complete yoga, is that which is taught by Self-Realization Fellowship, and which Bhagavan Krishna extols to his disciple Arjuna in the Bhagavad Gita: "The yogi is greater than body-disciplining ascetics, greater even than the followers of the path of wisdom or of the path of action; be thou, O Arjuna, a yogi!" (Bhagavad Gita VI:46). The sage Patanjali, foremost exponent of Yoga, has outlined eight definite steps by which the *Raja Yogi* attains *samadhi,* or union with God. These are (1) *yama,* moral conduct; (2) *niyama,* religious observances; (3) *asana,* right posture; (4) *pranayama,* control of *prana,* subtle life currents; (5) *pratyahara,* interiorization, withdrawal of the senses from external objects; (6) *dharana,* concentration, (7) *dhyana,* meditation; and (8) *samadhi,* superconscious experience; union with God.

yogi. One who practices Yoga *(q.v.).* Anyone who practices a scientific technique for divine realization is a yogi. He may be either married or unmarried, either a man of worldly responsibilities or one dedicated to formal religious vows.

Yogoda Satsanga Society of India. The name by which Paramahansa Yogananda's society is known in India. The Society was founded in 1917 by Paramahansa Yogananda. Its headquarters, Yogoda Math, is situated on the banks of the Ganges at Dakshineswar, near Calcutta. Yogoda Satsanga Society has a branch *math* at Ranchi, Jharkhand (formerly Bihar), and many branch centers. In addition to Yogoda meditation centers throughout India, there are twenty-two educational institutions, from primary through college level. *Yogoda,* a word coined by Paramahansa Yogananda, is derived from *yoga,* union, harmony, equilibrium; and *da,* that which imparts. "Satsanga" is composed of *sat,* truth, and *sanga,* fellowship. For the West, Sri Yogananda translated the Indian name as "Self-Realization Fellowship."

INDEX